THIS IS HAPPINESS:

MASTER YOUR MONEY, SPEND SMARTER, AND THRIVE IN LIFE

BEA ZELLY

ZATTI PRESS

WIN A FREE GIFT FROM US

Mastering your money and spending it smarter is key to thriving in life reaching your financial freedom. As a way of thanking you for buying our book, we would like to offer you a free gift, **a workbook for you to track your savings.** To grab it, please go to the link below:

My Free Savings Tracker Workbook

CONTENTS

INTRODUCTION

Can you imagine standing at the grocery store checkout with a cart full of items, and that nagging thought crosses your mind: "Can I really afford all this?" You've been good—putting in those extra hours, tightening the belt where you can—but somehow money just seems to burn holes in your pockets. It's like those crisp bills and shiny coins get restless when they're stuck in your wallet, always wanting to escape and find a new place to go. It could seem like they're practically begging to be spent, leaving you wondering how those hard-earned bills manage to disappear faster than a magician's rabbit. Maybe you'd like to ponder on that a bit more, but between juggling work, family, and free time (when you can get it), who has the energy? What if I told you there's a way to master your finances without becoming an accountant or turning into that person who counts every penny? Yes, even you can achieve this!

Money tends to be one of those taboos no one likes to discuss until they're knee-deep in debt or facing some unexpected emergency expense. But wouldn't it be refreshing if we approached it differently? Imagine how relieving it would be not having to count down the days until payday, knowing you're not scraping by until Friday. Instead of worrying about stretching every penny and counting down the hours, you can enjoy the freedom of having your finances under control, making the days between paychecks a breeze. The good news is, that understanding and taking control of your financial situation doesn't need to be more daunting than assembling flat-pack furniture.

How often do you feel that rush of blood pressure when you open your bank statement? Do you skim through it while holding your breath, hoping there's enough left after rent, utilities, and that unnecessary candle you bought last week (it was on sale, okay?). Financial awareness is truly the cornerstone of money management. Once you start recognizing where your income magically disappears to each month, making better choices becomes a lot easier. Think of it as shining a flashlight on the scary monster under your bed; once you see what you're dealing with, it's not so terrifying.

Here's where this book comes in as the guiding light that steers you away from financial missteps, offering you the tools and insights you need to navigate the often-confusing world of money management. It's designed to guide you, step by practical step, towards financial empowerment—no jargon that'll make your eyes glaze over, no complicated formulas that require a PhD to understand. This book promises straightforward advice, easy-to-use tools like apps, and practical tips that you can implement immediately. Each page is packed with little nuggets of wisdom aimed at helping you take charge of your budget and expenditure.

Let's be real: Starting your journey towards financial independence may seem like climbing Mount Fuji barefoot. Especially if budgeting is a foreign concept or you've always found yourself living paycheck to paycheck. It's okay; even the tallest oak started as a humble acorn. Each small step you take—from tracking your expenses to setting up a savings goal—is like laying down another cobblestone on your yellow brick road to self-sufficiency and inner peace. You don't need to become a master of finance overnight. Slow and steady wins the race, remember?

Financial freedom isn't just reserved for billionaires lounging on private yachts or celebrities with gold-plated credit cards. It's within reach for anyone willing to take the helm of their financial ship, navigating through budgeting and planning with a steady hand. It's like having your own key to a treasure chest—one that opens up to possibilities and peace of mind, regardless of your starting point. It's entirely within your reach, waiting there, like a well-lit path beckoning your way forward. Financial empowerment begins with simple changes and grows with consistency and dedication. And guess what? You'll begin to feel a different kind of thrill when you check your balance—not anxiety, but satisfaction and reassurance.

Wouldn't you like to flip through this book and feel the thrill of finding tips that not only steer you in the right direction but also light a fire in your belly? After all, a journey of a thousand miles begins with a single step. The concept of making sustainable choices isn't just an overused niche Instagram hashtag. Believe it or not, embracing minimalism or frugal living can bring immense satisfaction to your life, both financially and emotionally. Money in your pocket and emotional ease, who wouldn't sign up for that?

Think of how satisfying it would be to give the old heave-ho to the labyrinthine maze of financial jargon—those elusive, smoke-and-mirrors guidelines adorned with acronyms that seem to belong to an ancient script. Instead, welcome a realm of crystal-clear, actionable insights that illuminate your path, nurturing both your confidence and independence. Think of it as trading in a cryptic treasure map for a straightforward compass that offers guidance as transparent as a mountain spring, leading you with certainty toward your financial goals. Craft a mental snapshot of yourself gliding through a store, your cart effortlessly maneuvering through the aisles like a well-oiled machine. Each product you pick up is carefully considered, your decisions guided by a clear vision of exactly what you need. As you pass the sales racks, you scan them with the confidence of someone who knows their needs and goals, each choice made with purpose and ease. Now that's shopping prowess!

And let's face it, we could all use a bit more simplicity in our lives. This book is part of the larger *This is Happiness* series, setting a solid foundation for you to tackle other aspects of your life—like decluttering your space, practicing mindfulness, and much, much more. All these elements interconnect, creating a harmonious balance in your life that translates to greater happiness and satisfaction. Yes, it's possible to be financially savvy and zen at the same time. Balancing financial acumen with inner peace allows you to make decisions with both clarity and composure.

In embarking on this journey, you will uncover the power of choices, no matter how small they may seem. Every dollar saved and every unnecessary purchase avoided is a victory! This book is your blueprint, your compass guiding you through the maze of modern-day financial conundrums. By the end, you'll marvel at how far you've come. What once seemed overwhelming will transform into manageable, even enjoyable, tasks.

So, get ready to turn those defeated sighs into triumphant smiles. It's time to embrace a new approach to money, one that doesn't involve deprivation but encourages smarter choices. This book won't promise you instant riches because who needs another "get-rich-quick" scheme anyway? However, it will promise you something infinitely more valuable: Control over your spending, your saving, and ultimately, your financial destiny.

Get comfortable, grab a snack (a budget-friendly one, of course), and prepare to dive into a world where you can feel confident with every financial decision you make. Your journey to financial empowerment starts now, and trust me, you're going to love the destination.

UNIT 1: UNDERSTANDING YOUR FINANCIAL FOUNDATION

CHAPTER 1

ASSESSING YOUR CURRENT FINANCIAL SITUATION

Building a solid financial foundation means getting cozy with your income, expenses, and spending habits. Rather than thinking of it as a chore, imagine it as uncovering the hidden mysteries of your wallet—only less dusty and far more rewarding. This all starts by detecting exactly where your money is coming from; your mission is to become the Sherlock Holmes of your bank account. From the steady paycheck you earn at your nine-to-five job to the quirky little Etsy shop that brings in weekend dough, every source of income is a clue leading you toward financial stability.

Identifying All Sources of Income

Understanding your income is the first step in building a concrete financial foundation. By having a clear picture of where your money comes from, you can make informed decisions that will stabilize and grow your financial well-being. As the saying goes, "Know where your money flows, and you'll know how to make it grow."

First and foremost, let's talk about employment income. This is the most straightforward type of income for many people because it comes from their primary job. It's essential to keep tabs on everything you earn here, including your base salary, any overtime pay, and those nifty bonuses you might get for going above and beyond at work. Many folks forget about overtime and bonuses, treating them like extra money rather than part of their regular income. Recognizing these sources ensures you're not underestimating how much you actually have coming in each month.

But what happens when your primary job isn't the only source of income? Enter the world of freelance work and side hustles. With the gig economy booming, more and more people are turning to additional jobs or projects to supplement their primary income. Documenting all your freelance gigs, consulting work, or even that Etsy shop you run on the weekends is essential. Multiple income streams can offer financial security but only if you keep track of them. Use accounting software or apps to manage these varied earnings and ensure you're getting the bigger picture. Consistent documentation helps you understand which side hustles are worth your time and which ones aren't pulling their weight (Coinfella, 2023).

Next up is passive income. Wouldn't it be lovely to earn money while you sleep? That's the dream! Passive income can come from investments like stocks, bonds, or real estate rental properties. Don't overlook these sources just because they're not as hands-on as a traditional job. Calculate the dividends from your stock portfolio, the interest from your savings accounts, and the rent you collect from tenants. Tracking these income streams can add substantial value to your overall financial picture. And let's not forget passive income from digital products like eBooks or online courses you've created. These may require an initial time investment, but if you plant the seeds now, you'll reap the rewards for seasons to come.

Of course, life loves to throw us unexpected surprises, right? Occasionally, you might receive irregular payments that don't quite fit into the neat categories we've discussed. These could be unexpected bonuses from work, monetary gifts from family or friends, or even tax refunds. It's tempting to treat this money as a windfall and splurge on something fun, but for a solid financial foundation, you need to account for these, too. Document every penny and consider how these funds can best be used. Maybe toss them into an emergency fund or use them to pay off a bit of debt. Keeping track of these sources helps avoid surprises and maintains your financial equilibrium (Wong, 2016).

If you're starting in personal finance, it's easy to feel swamped by all these categories. But breaking them down makes the task manageable. Start with your primary job—get a handle on that salary, overtime, and bonuses. Then, move on to documenting your side hustles; once you've got that down, incorporate your passive income streams. Finally, be vigilant about those irregular, occasional payments. Little by little, you'll piece together a comprehensive picture of your financial inflow.

One practical approach is to set aside a fixed time each week to review and record all sources of income. This habit ensures nothing slips through the cracks. Additionally, using simple spreadsheets or financial apps can make this process less daunting. For example, apps like Mint or You Need a Budget (YNAB) allow you to visualize your income streams clearly, helping you stay organized and proactive about your finances (Holzhauer, 2021).

Now, don't think you have to handle this alone. If your financial situation is complex, consider consulting a financial advisor. They can provide professional guidance tailored to your unique circumstances, ensuring you maximize every penny you earn. Using professional help doesn't mean you're not good at managing money—it means you're smart enough to seek expert advice when needed.

Understanding your income is like laying a keystone for your financial future. When you know exactly how much money is coming in and from where, you can make informed decisions about saving, investing, and spending. When you see the path clearly, the journey to your financial dreams becomes a lot less daunting.

Tracking Your Daily Spending

Imagine sitting at a cozy café, latte in hand, and watching the world go by. You spot someone sitting nearby, diligently jotting down notes on their laptop and occasionally checking their phone. They're likely keeping track of their financial transactions, ensuring that every penny is accounted for. This scene highlights the concept of accountability in spending habits. Accountability in spending is the first brick in the house of financial security. By promoting mindful financial decisions, accountability allows you to understand where your money goes and how you can redirect it toward more significant priorities.

Maintaining a daily log of all expenses is your first step. Think of it as a personal diary, but instead of feelings and events, you're recording every coffee purchase, utility bill, and online shopping spree. When you write down every expense, no matter how small, you become keenly aware of your spending patterns. With time, clarity turns small steps into a clear path forward. Are those daily lattes adding up? Is there a recurring charge you've overlooked? Keeping this log isn't just about noting down amounts; it's about developing a habit of conscious spending. You're essentially training yourself to be more financially self-aware, which is a pillar of prudent money management.

Now, let's move beyond just logging expenses and talk about categorizing them. Expenses are like different flavors of ice cream. There's vanilla (essential groceries), chocolate (utilities), and maybe a quirky lavender (entertainment). When you sort your expenses into categories, you uncover the GPS signal to where your money is really headed. You could be overspending on dining out when you could be cooking at home. Or perhaps those subscription services you rarely use are eating into your budget more than you realized. Categorizing expenses helps pinpoint areas that need adjustment, making it easier to allocate funds wisely and avoid unnecessary expenditures.

Once you've got your categories set, analyzing your spending over time is the next logical step. It's like flipping through your old travel journals, where every entry tells the story of your journey and helps you plan the next adventure. Maybe there's a seasonal spike in spending during the holidays or a consistent dip in savings during the summer months. This helps you recognize problematic areas and make informed decisions.

But we don't live in the '90s anymore, so why not leverage modern tools to simplify this tracking process? Numerous apps are designed explicitly for expense tracking, each with its own unique features. Mint or Snoop simplifies personal finance by bringing all your accounts together, categorizing transactions, tracking spending, and creating custom budgets. With real-time alerts and an intuitive design, it keeps your finances in check effortlessly. YNAB turns every dollar into a purpose, prioritizing spending by goals and values. This proactive strategy helps break the paycheck-to-paycheck cycle and builds financial stability. YNAB is a key to tackling debt and saving for the future, guiding you toward financial independence (*The Importance of Expense Tracking*, n.d.).

These apps are just a few of many examples of how technology can assist in maintaining financial accountability. However, if you're not tech-savvy, don't worry! Simple methods like using a dedicated notebook or an Excel spreadsheet can be equally effective. The key is consistency. Whichever tool or method you choose, make it part of your daily routine. Just as you brush your teeth every morning, take a few minutes to review and record your expenses. Small habits today mean big rewards tomorrow!

Regular expense tracking is a proactive step toward financial stability. It helps you spot leaks, curb unnecessary spending, and build disciplined habits. Every journey starts with a single step—often just noting your expenses. So, as you enjoy that latte, consider if your spending aligns with your financial goals.

Pro Tips for Defining Financial Goals

Creating a roadmap to financial success involves setting clear, actionable goals that are aligned with your values and aspirations. It's like plotting a journey where each milestone brings you closer to financial security and peace of mind (von Aulock, 2024).

Establishing Short-Term Goals

Let's start with short-term goals, the small wins that set the stage for bigger achievements. These are objectives you aim to hit within a year or less. These quick wins can provide a tremendous sense of accomplishment, giving you the momentum to surmount bigger hurdles.

Why Quick Wins Matter

Quick wins pave the way for lasting financial habits. For instance, saving $500 for a mini-vacation might seem modest, but the budgeting skills you develop will serve you for years to come. Paying off small debts can be equally rewarding. It frees up mental space and financial resources, allowing you to focus on medium- and long-term goals without the nagging worry of those smaller liabilities.

Guidelines for setting short-term goals include:

- **Specific:** Define what you want to achieve clearly. Instead of "save money," set a target like "save $200 each month."

- **Measurable:** Track your progress. Use budgeting apps or simple spreadsheets to see how close you are to reaching your goal.

- **Achievable:** Ensure your goals are realistic given your current financial situation.

- **Relevant:** Make sure these goals align with your broader financial objectives.

- **Time-bound:** Set a deadline to keep yourself accountable.

Setting Medium-Term Goals

Medium-term goals span from one to five years and bridge the gap between the immediacy of short-term objectives and the far-off horizon of long-term dreams. Examples include saving for a car, putting together a down payment for a house, or paying off substantial student loans. These goals require more substantial planning and often a combination of saving and investing.

The Importance of Medium-Term Planning

Why should you bother with medium-term goals? Because they act as stepping stones toward your ultimate financial aspirations. Let's say you're saving up for a down payment on a home. This goal involves consistent monthly savings, perhaps cutting back on nonessential expenses and maybe even some strategic investments. In achieving this, you'll not only get closer to owning a home but also develop financial discipline and gain a deeper understanding of investment vehicles.

Guidelines for setting medium-term goals include:

- **Set priorities:** Determine which goals are most urgent and allocate resources accordingly.

- **Break down goals:** Divide large objectives into manageable tasks. If you're looking to save $20,000 in four years, aim for saving around $500 per month.

- **Stay flexible:** Life happens, and your priorities may shift. Be prepared to revisit and adjust your goals periodically.

- **Track progress:** Regularly check your advancement toward these goals and make necessary adjustments.

Creating Long-Term Goals

Long-term goals cover anything beyond five years. These could range from retirement savings to funding your child's education. These goals demand considerable planning, patience, and usually a more robust investment strategy.

Thinking Long-Term

Retirement might feel like a lifetime away, but the sooner you start preparing, the better. Similarly, if you're planning to send your kids to college, initiating a savings plan now can relieve future stress. Long-term goals often involve calculating how much you'll need and then working backward to determine how much you should save or invest annually.

Guidelines for setting long-term goals include:

- **Start early:** The earlier you begin, the more time your investments have to grow. Consider the power of compound interest over decades.

- **Consult experts:** For complex goals like retirement, professional advice can be invaluable. Financial advisors can help you create personalized plans and investment strategies.

- **Review annually:** Long-term goals should be reassessed every year to ensure they're still aligned with your life circumstances and market conditions.

- **Balance risks:** Diversify your investments to balance risks and rewards.

Aligning Goals with Values

While setting financial goals is paramount, aligning them with your personal values and life priorities can make them more meaningful and achievable. Why save for something that doesn't enrich your life or align with what you deeply care about?

Values-Based Goal Setting

Consider what's genuinely important to you. Is it financial independence? Being able to travel? Providing for your family? When your goals resonate with your values, you're more likely to stay committed to them, even when sacrifices are required.

If sustainability is a core value for you, consider directing your financial resources toward eco-friendly investments or savings. If community service is important, maybe part of your goal could be to donate to causes you care about or even volunteer financially to support local businesses.

Creating a Personal Financial Roadmap

Now, let's bridge these concepts together into a cohesive roadmap (von Aulock, 2024):

- **Identify your goals:** Write down all your short-, medium-, and long-term goals. Ensure they meet the SMART criteria (Specific, Measurable, Achievable, Relevant, Time-bound).

- **Categorize goals by time frames:** Separate your goals into short-term, medium-term, and long-term categories. This will help you prioritize.

- **Align with income and expenses:** Incorporate these goals into your financial plan. Map out how much of your income will go toward each goal and track your expenses to find areas where you can save more effectively.

- **Monitor and adjust:** Set regular intervals—monthly, quarterly, or annually—to review your goals. Adjust as needed to accommodate changes in your financial situation or life priorities.

Utilizing Tools and Resources

In the hurly burly of the modern world, building a solid financial foundation can often feel like trying to assemble a complex jigsaw puzzle without a clear picture. But, fear not! With the right tools and resources, managing your finances doesn't have to feel like swimming upstream.

First things first: Tracking your income and expenses accurately is crucial for financial success. Thankfully, several budgeting apps like the ones mentioned previously can make this process much easier. So, there's no need to stress over complicated spreadsheets—these apps will do the heavy lifting for you.

Next up, let's talk about financial calculators. These nifty tools can be incredibly helpful when planning your savings and investments. Websites like Money Saving Expert, Bankrate, and NerdWallet offer a variety of calculators that can assist with everything from figuring out your mortgage payments to planning for retirement. When you're eyeing a new loan, a loan calculator becomes your financial compass. It takes the guesswork out of how much you'll be paying each month by letting you explore various interest rates and loan terms. Planning for your child's college? A specialized calculator can forecast future tuition costs and show you how much you need to set aside each month. It's like having a personal guide to navigate your financial decisions. By taking advantage of these calculators, you can make informed decisions and avoid any unpleasant financial surprises down the road.

But wait, there's more! Financial literacy is the foundation upon which smart financial decisions are built. Fortunately, plenty of online courses and workshops are aimed at improving your financial knowledge. Platforms like Coursera, Udemy, and Khan Academy offer courses on various aspects of personal finance. For example, Coursera's "Finance for Everyone: Smart Tools for Decision-Making" developed by the University of Michigan is a great starting point (Williams, 2023). This self-paced course covers finance fundamentals and strategies for making good financial decisions. If you're looking for something more comprehensive, consider McGill University's "Personal Finance Essentials," which explores a wide range of topics including budgeting, investing, and retirement planning. And the best part? Many of these courses are free or very affordable, so you don't have to break the bank to become financially savvy.

Of course, sometimes there's no substitute for professional advice. Consulting with a financial advisor can provide you with personalized insights and recommendations tailored to your unique financial situation. Whether you're looking to invest, plan for retirement, or simply get a better handle on your budget, a financial advisor can guide you through the maze of options and help you develop a strategy that aligns with your goals. Advisors often have access to advanced software and tools that can analyze complex financial scenarios and present them in an easily digestible manner. They can also help ensure that your investment portfolio is diversified and aligned with your risk tolerance. Remember, it's important to choose an advisor who is reputable and has your best interests at heart, so do your homework and check their credentials before making a decision.

Final Insights

As we reflect on this chapter, we've rolled up our sleeves and dug deep into the nuts and bolts of understanding your income streams, keeping tabs on daily expenses, and grasping your spending patterns to lay a sturdy financial foundation. From your main gig and side hustles to those surprise windfalls, it's clear that every cent counts. Knowing exactly where your money is coming from and where it's going gives you the power to steer clear of those unexpected financial detours.

And let's talk about mindful spending for a moment. Tracking your expenses might sound like a chore, but think of it as journaling for your wallet—more clarity, less angst. Whether you jot down every coffee and cab ride or use sleek apps that do the heavy lifting, the aim is simple: to get a clear picture of your money habits. With this awareness, you can make smarter choices, tweak habits when needed, and get closer to those big dreams—whether it's snagging that perfect house or taking a much-deserved break.

Keep at it; each small step brings you closer to a stronger financial future. Next, we'll shift focus to the psychology of money, specifically how emotions and cultural influences shape our financial choices. This deeper understanding will help you develop a healthier relationship with money and make more informed decision.

CHAPTER 2

THE PSYCHOLOGY OF MONEY

Nurturing a positive relationship with money can feel like trying to do the merengue with an invisible partner—awkward and confusing. Many of us were never formally introduced to our financial feelings, leaving us to stumble through life making impulsive purchases and dodging overdue bills as if they were clingy exes stalking us in a grocery store. How many times have you found yourself stress-buying yet another pair of shoes or drowning your sorrows in the latest gadget? Yeah, me too. We often fail to realize that our wallets tend to follow our hearts more than our brains. Many are blissfully unaware of the emotional roller-coaster that drives spending habits, but recognizing these patterns can help us make smarter financial choices. So, grab your detective hat because we're about to investigate how our emotional triggers influence our decision-making at the cash register.

How Emotions Influence Spending Decisions

Understanding how emotions drive financial behaviors is key for those aiming to build a healthy relationship with money. Reflecting on our spending patterns reveals that emotional triggers often dictate our financial choices, leading to impulse purchases and other unwise decisions.

The Emotional Triggers Behind Impulse Purchases

Impulse purchases are frequently driven by emotional triggers. Stress-induced buying, where shopping becomes a coping mechanism during stressful times, is a common example (Marter, 2023). Boredom-driven spending can occur when we seek excitement or novelty in our lives. These kinds of purchases might bring a temporary reprieve, but they often lead to regret once the emotional high wears off. Recognizing these triggers is the first step toward controlling them.

- **Guideline:** To identify and manage these impulsive behaviors, one useful guideline is to implement the 24-hour rule. Before making any nonessential purchase, wait for a day. This delay can provide enough time to reconsider whether the purchase is genuinely necessary or just an emotional response (MAPFRE, 2023).

Guilt and Shame in Financial Decisions

Guilt and shame are the silent architects of our financial choices, shaping our behavior from the shadows. When people feel guilty about past financial mistakes, they may avoid dealing with their finances altogether, resulting in procrastination and exacerbating problems like debt accumulation. On the other hand, shame can lead to reckless spending as a way to escape feelings of inadequacy (Marter, 2023).

- **Guideline:** Reframing thoughts around money is essential for breaking this cycle. Viewing financial management as an empowering activity rather than a daunting task can shift one's mindset. Instead of dwelling on past errors, focus on small, achievable goals that promote positive actions. For instance, setting up automatic savings transfers can help build a sense of accomplishment and reduce financial stress.

How Happiness Is Connected to Financial Choices

Many believe that material possessions bring happiness, but true contentment often stems from experiences. Research suggests that investing in experiences like travel, concerts, or even simple gatherings with friends and family can create lasting joy (*Experiences Make People Happier*, 2004). These moments contribute to long-term well-being much more than fleeting satisfaction from buying the latest gadget or fashion item.

- **Guideline:** Prioritizing experiences over material goods requires a shift in perspective. It involves valuing memories and personal connections, which enhance life satisfaction more profoundly. Focusing on what brings genuine happiness helps you make more mindful financial decisions that align with your deeper values and aspirations.

Developing Emotional Awareness

Mastering your emotions is like holding the reins of a wild stallion; without it, your financial journey will inevitably veer off course. This involves recognizing and understanding the feelings that influence your spending habits. Take, for instance, someone who usually makes impulsive purchases whenever they're stressed. When they begin paying closer attention to their emotional triggers, they also begin to notice that these purchases often follow a pattern. For example, a rough day at work leads to an unplanned shopping spree. With this awareness, they can pause and reconsider their decisions, leading to more intentional spending choices.

- **Guideline:** Mindfulness exercises such as meditation or deep-breathing can provide clarity and emotional balance. When feeling overwhelmed by financial decisions, taking a moment to breathe and reflect can prevent hasty, emotion-driven actions (Fargo, 2024).

Examining How Culture Shapes Financial Habits

Cultural norms and values act as the unseen hand guiding our financial choices. These norms significantly influence financial behaviors, often leading people to follow the crowd rather than their own compass (Ahmed, 2021).

In certain cultures, money is seen as a symbol of success and power. A person raised in such an environment may feel pressured to accumulate wealth and demonstrate their financial status through visible displays like luxury cars, expensive clothes, or grand homes. Differentiating one's personal values from these societal expectations becomes essential. Someone may genuinely value financial security over material display but feels compelled to spend on items they don't necessarily need due to external pressure. Understanding this dynamic allows them to recognize these influences and make financial choices that truly resonate with their personal values rather than dictated by cultural norms.

Social media is the mirror that reflects an inflated image of wealth and success, distorting reality and complicating our financial aspirations. It's common to scroll through feeds filled with influencers flaunting lavish vacations, designer outfits, and opulent lifestyles, creating unrealistic benchmarks for everyday people. This kind of portrayal can lead to overspending and chronic dissatisfaction. The constant comparison can make one feel inadequate if their lifestyle doesn't match up to the curated images they see online. When faced with the temptation to buy the latest gadget, pause for a moment and asking yourself: "Do I need this, or am I just chasing after the image projected by social media?" This reflective pause can reveal whether the purchase is driven by a genuine need or merely by the urge to fit in with the latest trends. Recognizing the gap between online portrayals and reality is the first step to making more informed and gratifying financial decisions.

Family traditions around money also carry a substantial influence, often unconsciously shaping our current beliefs and habits. Growing up in a household where saving was prioritized can instill a strong sense of financial prudence. Conversely, if one's family frequently engaged in impulse buying, this habit might be carried into adulthood. Let's say you had a family tradition of celebrating every minor achievement with an extravagant gift growing up. This could create a habit of linking spending with emotional satisfaction. Redefining personal financial goals requires a conscious effort to identify these inherited habits and decide whether they align with your own values. Someone who grew up in a spendthrift environment might benefit from setting new boundaries, like focusing on saving for long-term goals rather than immediate gratifications (Ross, 2013).

Community and societal influences further shape our spending and saving attitudes. The social circles we move in can either support or derail our financial discipline. Being part of a community that highly values frugality and sustainable living can reinforce positive financial behaviors. On the other hand, if one's social group indulges in regular high-end dining and impulsive shopping sprees, the pressure to fit in can lead to unhealthy financial choices. Assessing one's social circle is vital for better financial behaviors. Surrounding oneself with individuals who share similar financial goals, such as saving for retirement or investing wisely, creates a supportive environment that encourages prudent decision-making.

Pro Tips for Breaking Negative Spending Patterns

Spotting those sneaky spending habits is like finding the leak in a sinking ship—ignore it, and you might as well start practicing your backstroke. The first step is to identify your personal spending triggers. These triggers are often tied to emotions like stress, boredom, or even celebration (Roth, 2018).

Keeping a Spending Journal

To uncover these emotional connections, journaling practices can be incredibly effective. By keeping a journal of your spending habits, you can start to recognize patterns and understand the underlying emotions that drive your purchases. Jotting down how you felt before and after each transaction can reveal if you're using shopping as an emotional crutch. You might notice that you feel anxious before buying and momentarily satisfied afterward. This practice promotes self-awareness and enables you to bring about lasting change.

Clearing the Clutter

Building a network of encouragement and accountability is key to overcoming harmful financial habits. Removing shopping apps from your smartphone and unsubscribing from promotional emails can reduce temptation significantly. An inbox free from sales alerts and a phone without ads is a rare treasure. It's like decluttering your mind from unnecessary noise, allowing you to focus on what truly matters. You could go a step further by not saving your credit card information on websites. Each manual entry can act as a moment to reconsider the purchase, potentially saving you from impulsive buys. Sure, it's a bit inconvenient, but that's precisely the point—it creates a pause to reflect on whether you really need that item.

The 30-Day Rule

Implementing the 30-day rule is another excellent strategy to differentiate between true needs and impulse buys. When you find something you think you must have, note it down and revisit it 30 days later. If you still feel the same about it after this period, then consider making the purchase. Often, you'll find that the initial excitement has waned, and what's left is a clearer perspective on whether the item is necessary. This rule helps instill patience and thoughtfulness, countering the instant gratification that modern shopping often provides. It's like giving yourself the gift of time to decide wisely.

Finding Healthier Alternatives

Developing alternative coping mechanisms can offer healthier emotional responses compared to retail therapy. Engaging in non-financial activities like exercise, hobbies, or quality time with loved ones can serve as fulfilling substitutes. For instance, if you typically shop online to unwind after a stressful day, try going for a run or practicing some yoga instead. Physical activity releases endorphins, which naturally boost your mood. Alternatively, picking up a hobby like painting, reading, or gardening can provide a similar sense of accomplishment and satisfaction without the financial cost. These alternatives not only divert your mind from shopping but also contribute positively to your overall well-being.

Setting Clear Financial Goals

It's also beneficial to set clear financial goals. Knowing why you want to cut back on spending can be a powerful motivator. Whether it's saving for a vacation, paying off debt, or simply wanting to build a more secure financial future, having a tangible goal in mind makes it easier to stick to your plans. Write down your goals and keep them visible, perhaps on your fridge or near your computer. Every time you're tempted to make an unnecessary purchase, these reminders can help steer you back on track.

Tracking Your Spending

Tracking your spending is another effective method to gain control over your finances. When you monitor every dollar spent, you often realize just how much money goes toward nonessential items. Highlighting these expenses on your bank statements can put things into perspective, showing you areas where you can cut back. You might even calculate how many hours of work are required to afford those purchases, making the impact of your spending more tangible. This exercise isn't about taking a guilt trip; it's about driving awareness and steering you towards more deliberate spending.

Sometimes, our spending habits are influenced by deeper psychological factors rooted in our upbringing or past experiences. Reflecting on these aspects can be revealing. Maybe money was scarce growing up, leading you to splurge when you finally had a steady income. Or perhaps you've always had enough and never learned the value of restraint. Understanding these underlying motivations can help you reframe your relationship with money, fostering healthier habits.

It's also important to recognize that changing your spending habits won't happen overnight. It's a gradual process marked by small victories and occasional bumps along the way. Be kind to yourself and avoid harsh judgment when you slip up. The goal is to make sustainable changes, and that requires patience and persistence. Celebrate your progress, no matter how small, and use each setback as an opportunity to bounce back.

If managing your spending feels like wrestling with a grizzly, consider reaching out for support from friends, family, or even professional counselors. Sometimes, external perspectives can provide valuable insights and encouragement. Joining online communities or support groups focused on personal finance can also offer a sense of camaraderie and shared purpose. Remember, you're not alone in this journey, and seeking help is a sign of strength, not weakness.

Final Insights

Addressing emotional triggers and cultural influences is a powerful step toward better financial habits. Recognizing that stress, boredom, guilt, and shame often drive our spending can help us manage these impulses more effectively. By implementing practical strategies and pro tips mentioned in this chapter, you pave the way for more mindful decisions. Embracing small, achievable goals rather than dwelling on past mistakes transforms financial management into an empowering exercise.

Understanding cultural norms and family traditions is like having a map that guides you through the maze of societal pressures with clarity. Whether it's resisting the temptations of social media or redefining personal goals that align with our true values, awareness is key. Establishing a supportive environment and seeking professional advice when needed builds a balanced approach to money, grounded in emotional awareness and cultural understanding. This journey may be gradual, but with patience and persistence, we can make sustainable changes that lead to lasting financial well-being.

Now that we've unpacked how our emotions and cultural influences shape our financial habits, it's time to get hands-on. The next chapter, 'The Basics of Budgeting,' will introduce you to essential budgeting methods and techniques. These tools will help you build a strong foundation for financial stability and make your financial goals more achievable.

CHAPTER 3

THE BASICS OF BUDGETING

Effective budgeting is like taming a wild beast—it's not glamorous, but it can save you from financial doom. Now, let's say you're the zookeeper of your finances, trying to keep everything from eating each other alive. Without a solid budget, your money will run wild, gnawing at your sanity and chomping on your dreams of that European vacation or early retirement. But with just a bit of planning and discipline, you can turn that financial menagerie into a well-organized exhibit, where every penny knows its place.

The Role of Budgeting in Financial Stability

Let's talk about budgeting, the financial superhero you didn't know you needed. So, you're piloting a spaceship called "personal finances" through the treacherous galaxy of expenses, debts, and savings goals. Without a budget, you're basically flying blindfolded. But with one? Congratulations, you've got yourself a navigational tool so powerful it could make Han Solo eat his heart out.

First up, let's consider how budgeting acts as your guiding star in the vast expanse of personal finances. Think of it like Google Maps but for money. Input your income and expenses, and voila! You have a clear route to follow—no more wandering aimlessly in the black hole of "Where did all my money go?" Instead, you'll chart a course through paydays, bills, and even spontaneous donut cravings with the precision of a seasoned explorer. Budgeting involves more than just restricting spending; it focuses on prioritizing where your hard-earned money should go to give you the most significant financial bang for your buck. You wouldn't drive a car without knowing your destination, right? So why treat your finances any differently?

A well-structured budget can prevent overspending while boosting your savings account from sad single digits to something that would make Scrooge McDuck envious. When you outline specific categories—like food, entertainment, housing, and emergency funds—you create boundaries that curb impulse buying (sorry, late-night Amazon shopping sprees). This structure gives every penny a purpose, from paying off debt to fueling your car or saving for your next summer vacation.

Budgeting also brings an improvement in overall financial wellness by shining a light on your spending patterns. A budget helps you detect areas where money might be slipping through the cracks unnoticed. Maybe you're spending a suspicious amount on artisanal cupcakes or have a gym membership that's collecting dust. Identifying these habits gives you the power to change them, reallocating funds to more critical areas like savings or investments. Over the long haul, these small shifts add up, leading to massive improvements in your financial stability.

Knowing your expenses are managed gives you greater control over your financial future. A unique kind of peace comes from knowing exactly where your money goes each month. It removes the anxiety of unexpected expenses and allows you to plan for the future confidently. You become the master of your financial destiny rather than its hapless victim. That's the power of feeling financially secure.

Now, I know what you're thinking: Budgeting sounds about as much fun as watching paint dry. But it doesn't have to be a dreary task. You can gamify the process, turning saving and spending into a challenge rather than a chore. Set monthly goals and reward yourself for sticking to them. Use apps that turn budgeting into a visual experience with charts and progress trackers. You might find it oddly satisfying to see those expense bars shrink while your savings skyrocket.

One fascinating aspect is how budgeting forces you to confront your priorities head-on, distinguishing between needs and wants. Let's face it, we've all blurred those lines at some point. But a budget makes it clear: Rent and groceries, for example, are non-negotiable needs, while a new video game or designer handbag falls squarely into the "want" category. This clarity helps you allocate resources efficiently, ensuring your essentials are covered first. What's left can then be divided between savings and discretionary spending. This simple clarity transforms the way you handle money, reducing waste and promoting smarter choices.

What's more, having a structured budget creates a sense of accountability. It's like having a financial coach who keeps you honest. Regularly reviewing your budget isn't about self-shaming but understanding your financial behavior. Did you stray from your budget this month? No worries; revisit your plan, adjust, and get back on track. This practice instills discipline and encourages responsible habits, leading to long-term financial health. Of course, flexibility is key. Life happens, and budgets need to adapt. Maybe an unexpected medical bill surfaces, or you decide to switch careers. A robust budget isn't rigid; it evolves with your circumstances, offering a life raft in turbulent waters.

Effective budgeting also creates opportunities for strategic savings. By earmarking funds for specific goals—whether it's a dream vacation, a home down payment, or an emergency fund—you ensure these priorities aren't left to chance. Watching your savings blossom provides tangible proof of your progress, reinforcing positive financial behavior. These savings give you options, allowing greater flexibility and security in life's decisions.

Identifying Essential vs. Nonessential Expenses

A wise budget knows the difference between what keeps you afloat and what makes the voyage enjoyable. Distinguishing needs from wants is the foundation that keeps your budget standing tall and your stress levels low.

Defining Essential Expenses

Number one on our list: essential expenses. These are the basics that you simply cannot live without, like:

- **Housing:** The rent or mortgage payments keeping a roof over your head.

- **Food:** The groceries filling your fridge.

- **Transportation:** The gas that gets you to work.

Imagine life without paying these; it's a highway to having your electricity cut off or camping out in your car—not exactly the road trip you were thinking about. Housing costs, such as rent or mortgage payments, are usually fixed and predictable, making them easier to plan for. Daily necessities like food and groceries, while they can vary, still fall under essential spending because hunger isn't picky about the budget. Understanding your essential needs can help prioritize spending and optimize budget planning.

Clarifying Nonessential Expenses

Ah, yes, nonessential expenses, those delightful little things that make life enjoyable but aren't strictly necessary for survival. We're talking about entertainment, dining out, and hobbies. Ever thought about how much of your paycheck goes towards binge-watching subscriptions or that just-one-more-time sushi dinner? Clarifying what falls into this category helps pinpoint areas where you can cut back without spiraling into hopelessness.

Identifying these costs can illuminate areas where spending can be reined in without sacrificing joy. So, when your budget feels like it's wearing a bit thin, trading the clink of glasses at a swanky restaurant for the sizzle of a stovetop at home can keep your wallet full without dimming the laughter around the dinner table. The goal isn't to strip away all pleasure but to recognize where adjustments can be made to free up funds for what's truly important.

Creating a Balance

Striking a balance between essential and nonessential expenses ensures you're not only meeting your basic needs but also enjoying life. Creating a balance involves understanding how to allocate funds proportionately. Not every dollar needs a strict label, though. Some fluidity can help—think adjusting your dining-out budget when an unexpected car repair comes up. When times are good, you can indulge more in discretionary spending. When they're not, you have a clear picture of where to tighten the belt.

Budget Categorization Tools

Budget categorization tools are your best friends here. Whether you prefer an old-school spreadsheet or a snazzy app, these tools help you keep tabs on where your money goes. They provide a visual breakdown, making it easier to spot trends and leaks in your budget. For those who love color-coding (you know who you are), these tools can turn budgeting into a surprisingly satisfying task.

Ultimately, separating necessary costs from luxuries enhances spending accountability. This doesn't mean you should feel guilty about every latte or movie ticket; rather, it encourages mindful spending. By being aware of where your money is going, you can make conscious choices that align with your financial goals.

Let's say you want to save for a vacation. Knowing that your essential expenses are covered first lets you see how much you can realistically set aside each month. Maybe that's cutting a couple of streaming services or skipping artisanal coffees. The key is to find a balance that doesn't force you into a life of Spartan deprivation but allows some flexibility to enjoy the present while planning for the future.

Balancing Needs and Wants in Your Spending

Imagine you're at a fancy buffet with endless options. There's filet mignon on one side and a mountain of chocolate éclairs on the other. Your wallet is your plate, and you must choose wisely to satisfy both your hunger and sweet tooth without bursting or breaking the bank. Welcome to the world of budgeting, where distinguishing between needs and wants is like mastering the art of juggling flaming swords while riding a unicycle.

Understanding the difference between needs and wants is the key to healthy budgeting. Needs are the essentials—the meat and potatoes of your financial diet. These include housing, utilities, food, clothing, healthcare, and transportation. They're non-negotiable; without them, it's "Goodbye Mr. Chips". On the flip side, wants are the truffle oil drizzle on your budget pizza—nice to have but not critical for survival.

When it comes to mindful spending practices, think of yourself as a vigilant shepherd guarding your flock of dollars. Mindful spending involves taking a moment before each purchase to ask, "Is this a need or a want?" If it's a need, proceed with confidence. If it's a want, dig deeper. Does it align with your values and goals? Will it bring lasting satisfaction or instant regret? By prioritizing needs over wants and evaluating each purchase, you can turn impulse buying into intentional investing in your happiness.

Aligning your spending with your financial goals is like having a GPS for your money—without it, you'll get hopelessly lost in a jungle of receipts and regret. Let's say you want to buy a house, pay off debt, or take a dream vacation. These goals ask you to sharpen your financial instincts, steering your resources toward what truly counts. Each dollar you spend should act as a building block toward these larger goals. Opting for home-cooked meals over dining out frequently can free up funds for your travel savings. As you see these savings accumulate, the sense of accomplishment can be far more rewarding than the fleeting joy of an expensive meal.

But life isn't a yellow brick road paved with gold and good intentions. It's a wild rollercoaster with unexpected twists and turns. Hence, flexibility in financial planning is key. Being adaptable means having Plan B (and C, D, and E) when unforeseen circumstances throw a wrench into your meticulously laid plans. Flexibility encourages resilience, allowing you to recover quickly from setbacks. When your car decides to impersonate a lawnmower mid-commute, having the wiggle room in your budget to cover repairs can prevent financial derailment. Creating a flexible budget means periodically reviewing and adjusting your spending categories to reflect changes in your income, expenses, or goals.

Incorporating tools and templates into your budgeting process can be a game-changer. Imagine trying to assemble IKEA furniture without those little hex keys and confusing diagrams. Chaos, right? In the same way, budgeting without tools is bound to end in frustration. Simple budgeting worksheets can act as your hex keys, helping you map out and categorize expenses. Digital tools like budgeting apps offer real-time insights and notifications, keeping you accountable and aware of your spending habits. These tools can streamline the process, making it easier to stick to your plan and adapt as needed.

Budget categorization is another effective strategy (Blaine, 2024). Categorizing your budget helps create clarity and order, ensuring you don't mix up your grocery money with your Netflix subscription. Breaking down your expenses into specific categories such as housing, food, entertainment, and savings allows for better tracking and analysis. You'll quickly identify areas where you might be overspending and where there's room for adjustment.

Your budget needs regular check-ups and tweaks to keep your financial peace intact. Just as you wouldn't wear the same pair of shoes forever, your budget needs periodic updates. Monthly or quarterly reviews help gauge your progress and make necessary tweaks. Are you meeting your savings goals? Is there an increase in an expense category? This habit of regular check-ins ensures that your budget remains a living, breathing document that evolves with your changing circumstances.

Achieving harmony between financial necessities and personal desires requires constant vigilance, thoughtful decision-making, and an adaptability mindset.

It's about finding that sweet spot where responsible spending meets fulfilling experiences. With a clear understanding of needs versus wants, mindful spending, goal alignment, and flexible planning, you can navigate the treacherous waters of personal finance with the grace of a seasoned sailor. Tools and regular reviews ensure you stay on course, ready to adjust your sails as needed.

Pro Tips for Setting Up Your First Budget

Before you can start budgeting, you need to gather all necessary financial information. Grab those ancient scrolls (also known as pay stubs) and jot down your income sources. Include everything, from your regular paycheck to irregular incomes like freelancing gigs or that crisp $20 dollar bill you found in your winter coat pocket. But don't let it go to your head; humility is key!

Next, you'll want to identify both fixed and variable expenses. Fixed expenses are like that loyally annoying friend who shows up at your house unannounced—rent, utilities, car payments—they're always there and they never change. Variable expenses, on the other hand, are like fair-weather friends. These include groceries, dining out, and the occasional splurge on a new pair of shoes you didn't really need but convinced yourself were essential.

Now, once you've collected all this juicy data, you're ready to reflect on your financial habits and preferences. Do you have a penchant for lattes? Is online shopping your guilty pleasure? Understanding your spending personality is crucial when choosing a budgeting method. You wouldn't use a key that doesn't fit the lock, right? So why use a method that doesn't suit your lifestyle?

Once you've chosen a budgeting method that matches your habits and preferences, it's time to establish some financial goals. Use the SMART criteria: Specific, Measurable, Achievable, Relevant, and Time-bound. For example, rather than saying, "I want to save money," say, "I want to save $500 in three months for an emergency fund." This kind of clarity not only motivates you but also provides a clear pathway to achieving your goal.

Think of setting short-term and long-term goals as planting seeds in your financial garden. Short-term goals might include saving for holiday gifts or reducing credit card debt, whereas long-term goals could involve buying a home or investing for retirement. And don't forget about that rainy day fund! Life has a way of throwing curveballs—be prepared with an emergency fund that can cover unexpected expenses like medical bills or car repairs.

Now, here comes the fun part: implementing your budget. Keep track of your spending religiously. Use apps like Snoop, YNAB, Rocket Money, Quicken Simplifi, or Empower to monitor your expenses. Many banks offer complimentary online budgeting services which can alert you if you've gone over budget in specific categories. The idea is to keep an eagle-eye on your spending patterns and adjust accordingly.

Just like any living entity, your budget isn't static. It's a dynamic, ever-evolving organism that needs constant care and attention. Regularly review and adjust your budget to ensure it aligns with your changing financial situation. Did you get a raise? Great! Adjust your savings and investment percentages. Or maybe an unexpected expense came up? Time to tighten the belt on discretionary spending.

Review your budget at least once a month. Ask yourself critical questions: Are you meeting your financial goals? Are there areas where you consistently overspend? Are your priorities shifting? By frequently reviewing your budget, you can make the necessary tweaks to stay on track and avoid financial pitfalls.

Finally, celebrate your small victories. Sticking to a budget can feel like swimming upstream, and it's okay to reward yourself for milestones reached. Just make sure your rewards don't take you off course. A little treat now and then won't hurt as long as it fits within your budget.

Final Insights

To sum up, understanding essential budgeting techniques is like unlocking a secret level in the game of life. We've explored how a budget can be your financial GPS, guiding you through the labyrinth of expenses, savings, and even those sneaky little donut cravings. By categorizing your spending into needs, wants, and savings, you prioritize your hard-earned cash more effectively than ever before. Whether you're aiming for a hefty savings account or just trying to dodge impulsive buys, these budgeting tools offer frameworks to help you stay on course.

Let's not pretend budgeting is all rainbows and unicorns; it's more like taming a wild beast with a spreadsheet and a calculator. Once you've got it under control, you're no longer at the mercy of surprise expenses or random splurges. You're the captain of your financial ship, equipped with an emergency fund and strategic savings goals. It emphasizes making mindful choices that align with your values and long-term objectives, turning financial chaos into peace of mind. So, embrace your inner budgeting Buzz Lightyear and steer your spaceship towards a stable financial future!

Now that you've got a handle on the basics of budgeting and its role in achieving financial stability, it's time to take the next step. In the upcoming chapter, we'll focus on building a comprehensive budget. I'll walk you through creating a detailed and flexible plan that covers all your financial needs and goals, helping you take control of your money and set yourself up for lasting success.

UNIT 1: RESOURCES AND TOOLS

Financial calculators:
- Money Saving Expert

- Bankrate

- NerdWallet

Online courses and workshops:
- Coursera

- Udemy

- Khan Academy

Financial apps:
- Snoop

- Rocket Money

- Quicken Simplifi

- Empower

- You Need a Budget (YNAB)

- Goodbudget

UNIT 2: CREATING A PERSONALIZED BUDGET

CHAPTER 4

BUILDING A COMPREHENSIVE BUDGET

Creating a detailed and flexible budget is as exciting and challenging as trying to master the perfect recipe while juggling flaming maracas, but it's necessary for financial peace. It's about more than just jotting down numbers and hoping for the best. Instead, think of it as designing a roadmap where every penny has a designated pit stop, yet there's room for unexpected detours without sending you into a fiscal frenzy. Done right, this kind of budgeting allows you to cover all your essentials while still having room for those little luxuries that make life worth living.

Exploring Various Budgeting Techniques

There you are, sitting with your morning coffee, contemplating how you'll wrestle your finances into submission. Worry not, for I am about to introduce some budgeting techniques that might just become your new best friends (Luthi, 2020).

The Envelope System

First, the Envelope System is a tried-and-true technique that predates online banking. Here's how it works: You label physical envelopes for different spending categories like groceries, entertainment, and dining out. Each envelope gets filled with cash according to your allocated budget for that category. When the money's gone, it's gone—simple as that. This method curbs impulsive purchases because nothing says "no" like an empty envelope. It offers direct control over spending, making you reconsider that fourth latte or impromptu shoe purchase. And for those of you who don't relish carrying a wad of cash around, there are digital versions of this method too. Apps like Goodbudget mimic the envelope system without the risk of losing envelopes under your couch cushions. This method shines brightest for anyone striving for financial discipline by sticking strictly to their plans.

50/30/20 Rule

Next, we have the 50/30/20 rule, a budgeting classic. Your finances are divided into three categories: needs, wants, and savings or debt repayment. The beauty of this method is its simplicity. You allocate 50% of your income to necessities like rent, groceries, and utilities. These are the non-negotiables, the pillars holding up your life. Next, 30% goes to discretionary spending—think dinners out, streaming subscriptions, or that robot vacuum you've been eyeing. This is where your fun money resides. Finally, 20% is earmarked for savings and debt repayment. Whether you're building an emergency fund or tackling student loans, this slice of your budget works toward securing your financial future. Remember, deviations from these percentages are okay if it helps meet your financial goals. Flexibility is key, and the 50/30/20 rule offers just that.

Zero-Based Budgeting (ZBB)

While the 50/30/20 rule is excellent for those who prefer a straightforward approach, some of us need to be more hands-on. That's where the Zero-Based Budgeting (ZBB) comes in. This method is all about giving every bit of your income a job. At the end of the month, your income minus expenses should equal zero. No, you don't have to devour ramen noodles until your next payday—it's more about meticulous planning. Every expense, no matter how small, is accounted for. From your rent to that jar of pickles you craved at midnight, everything has its place. ZBB is ideal for eliminating debt or achieving specific savings targets since you're tracking every dime closely. For those who love spreadsheets or apps, this method was created for you.

The Pay-Yourself-First Budgeting Technique

The pay-yourself-first budgeting method is like being the boss of your money, with a firm but fair "salary negotiation" between your paycheck and your priorities. You start by giving your savings and debt repayment their cut first—because they're like the star employees who keep the whole operation running. The rest of the funds can then go to everything else, like paying for groceries or the inevitable Friday night takeout that always seems like a good idea. Instead of putting off savings until the end of the month, when your wallet is emptier than your motivation on a Monday morning, you automate those transfers. It's a bit like setting up a direct deposit to your future, and it means you don't have to agonize over every little expense. By keeping things simple, you're more likely to stick to it, and your savings get to grow while you're busy doing literally anything else.

Incorporating these diverse budgeting methods into your financial toolkit can transform how you manage money, each offering unique advantages suited to varying lifestyles and preferences.

Preparing for Unexpected Expenses

Planning for unforeseen financial challenges is like having an umbrella on a cloudy day—you might not need it, but you'll be glad it's there when the storm hits. Let's get down to the nitty-gritty of how you can save your financial well-being from the cold fronts of unexpected expenses.

Understanding the Nature of Unexpected Expenses

If only life were as predictable as binge-watching a corny B-grade TV show. Sadly, it doesn't work that way. Your car may throw a tantrum with a surprise need for repairs, or your pet stages a sudden, dramatic audition for a vet commercial by eating something bizarre. These costs aren't part of your monthly grocery list but have an uncanny knack for showing up uninvited.

Being blindsided by these financial curveballs isn't inevitable. You can arm yourself with knowledge about common unexpected expenses: medical bills, major home repairs, and emergency travel. Knowing what could hit helps you prepare better. Plus, it makes you feel like a finance wizard who saw it all coming!

Building an Emergency Fund

An emergency fund is like a financial safety net, except it's less circus, more stability. Having this buffer means not having to borrow from your future self (who's already stressed out enough).

So, how do you build one? Saving even a little bit each month can snowball over time into a robust emergency fund. Divide your paycheck so a portion automatically goes into savings. Out of sight, out of mind. And no, it's not just about stashing cash in your sock drawer. Consider putting your emergency funds in a high-yield savings account—safe yet accessible.

Aim for at least three to six months' worth of living expenses (Anderson, n.d.). This might sound like climbing Mount Everest, but take it one step at a time. Just like Rome wasn't built in a day, neither is a solid emergency fund. Regular contributions—even small ones—add up faster than you think.

Building an emergency fund is a smart move, and plenty of apps and websites can help you stash away that safety net. Here are some tools to consider:

- **Acorns:** Acorns rounds up your everyday purchases to the nearest dollar and invests the spare change. It's a hassle-free way to slowly build your emergency fund while investing for the future.

- **Qapital:** Qapital helps you save money by setting up custom savings goals and automating contributions based on your spending habits or specific rules you set (like saving $5 every time you buy coffee). It's like having a financial fairy godmother.

- **Digit:** Digit analyzes your spending patterns and automatically transfers small amounts from your checking account to your Digit savings account. It's like having a personal savings assistant who's always watching out for you.

- **Chime:** Chime offers a savings account with automatic round-ups and a feature that transfers a percentage of your paycheck directly into your savings. It's straightforward and user-friendly, helping you save without even thinking about it.

Insurance Considerations

Insurance is like hiring bodyguards for your bank account. Different types of insurance—health, auto, home—can shield you from getting sucker-punched by sudden expenses.

Don't consider it a mere formality; think of it as a necessary precaution. Health insurance can mitigate the sting of those steep medical bills. Auto insurance can cover a good chunk of those surprising car repairs. Home insurance can help when your house decides to spring a leak or invite termites for dinner.

Before you say, "But insurance is just another expense," remember that it's an investment. It's better to pay a little now than a lot later. Your future self will thank you while sipping a piña colada on an impromptu beach vacation made possible by not being knee-deep in debt.

Flexible Budget Adjustments

Even the best-laid plans need wiggle room. Let's be honest: No budget is ironclad. A flexible budget is like yoga for your finances—it bends without breaking.

When unexpected expenses rear their ugly heads, don't resist adjusting your budget. Flexibility here is key. Start by identifying nonessential spending. Redirect those funds to cover the surprise costs. Your budget is a rubber band—it stretches but snaps back. Adapting your financial plan isn't admitting defeat; it's showcasing resilience. This approach ensures you stay on track without detailing your long-term goals.

Pro Tips to Keep Your Budget on Its Toes

Understanding is one thing; implementing is another. Here are some actionable strategies:

- **Track everything:** Use budgeting apps to keep tabs on every dollar. Knowing where your money goes helps you spot areas to cut back when needed.

- **Set priorities:** Rank your expenses. Essentials first, nonessentials second. This hierarchy becomes invaluable when you need to make swift budget changes.

- **Review regularly:** Monthly budget reviews aren't fun, but they're vital. Adjust as you go to ensure you're prepared for any surprises.

- **Emergency drills:** Conduct hypothetical scenarios. What if the car breaks down? What if there's a sudden trip to the ER? Practicing these drills helps you react calmly when real emergencies strike.

The aim here isn't to turn you into a paranoid penny-pincher but a savvy spender. Balance is everything. Enjoy life—just not at the cost of your financial health. Knowing you've got an emergency fund, proper insurance, and a flexible budget helps you sleep easier.

Avoiding Common Budgeting Blunders

Budgeting might seem like a no-brainer, but even the best intentions can go awry. Let's steer clear of the most common budgeting blunders:

- **The "I'll just wing it" approach:** Ah, the classic move of pretending your finances will magically work themselves out. Spoiler alert: They won't. Ignoring irregular expenses like annual subscriptions or surprise vet bills is like forgetting to pack an umbrella during a monsoon. Plan ahead, or prepare for a soggy wallet.

- **Underestimating variable costs:** Variable expenses are the financial equivalent of a mystery box—groceries one week, impulse Amazon buys the next. Keeping track of these sneaky expenditures can feel like herding cats, but a little vigilance goes a long way. Don't let your budget be a guessing game—get precise or risk a surprise raid on your savings.

- **Setting unrealistic goals:** Sure, we all dream of winning the lottery, but aiming for a budget so tight you can't afford to breathe isn't sustainable. Set realistic goals that won't have you living on ramen noodles and regret. Small, achievable steps are the secret to long-term success—and less stress over what's for dinner.

- **Neglecting to track spending:** Think of your expenses as that pesky dust you always forget to clean. If you don't track your spending, it'll pile up until you're drowning in financial grime. Whether you're using an app or a good old-fashioned ledger, keep tabs on where your money is going. Otherwise, you might find yourself asking, "Where did all my money go?" while eyeing your empty wallet.

- **Forgetting to adjust for lifestyle changes:** Life changes faster than a chameleon on a rainbow, and your budget needs to keep up. Got a new job, a bigger house, or a growing family? Adjust your budget accordingly—or face the consequences of a surprise financial faceplant. Keep your budget flexible and in sync with your ever-evolving life.

- **Failing to plan for savings:** Treat savings like a VIP guest at your financial party. If you don't make room for it, you'll end up with a half-empty dance floor and no cushion for emergencies. Allocate funds for savings as if you're paying for premium party favors—because future-you will thank you for the thoughtful planning.

- **Overlooking emotional spending:** We all know that one impulse buy can be as tempting as a donut in a diet. Emotional spending can derail even the most disciplined budget. Recognize when you're splurging to soothe a bad day and redirect those feelings into something less costly, like yoga, a walk, or a Netflix binge.

By avoiding these classic budgeting missteps, you'll be on your way to financial sanity with a bit of humor to lighten the load. Remember, budgeting doesn't have to be a drag; it's your personal finance adventure, complete with its own set of amusing challenges and triumphs.

Positioning Budgeting as a Life Skill

Mastering the art of budgeting is akin to possessing a superpower, one that will help you confidently tackle financial villains and enhance your financial literacy. A well-structured budget is a blueprint, helping you manage expenses, income, and saving goals effectively. By setting specific limits on spending and ensuring money is allocated towards savings and debt repayment, you can avoid the common pitfalls of overspending and develop a sense of control over your finances. This proactive approach not only reduces stress but also prepares you for unexpected financial hurdles such as emergency medical expenses or job loss.

Understanding economic fluctuations through budgeting cultivates a positive financial mindset. The economy can be as unpredictable as a kite in a storm, but budgeting helps you weather these ups and downs. Knowledge is power, and being informed allows you to make strategic adjustments to your budget during times of economic uncertainty. For instance, during periods of inflation, you might prioritize increasing your savings or cutting back on nonessential spending. This mindset shift from reactive to proactive financial planning builds resilience and adaptability, crucial traits for long-term financial success. Commitment to budgeting encourages lifelong financial responsibility and accountability. It's easy to get swept up in the allure of instant gratification. However, a consistent budgeting practice teaches discipline and prioritization. When you continuously monitor and adjust your budget, you learn to set realistic financial goals and work diligently towards them.

Cultivating mindful spending habits contributes to a balanced lifestyle and long-term financial success. In today's consumer-driven world, it's easy to fall into the trap of mindless spending. But budgeting helps you become more intentional with your money. Categorizing expenses—essentials, nonessentials, and savings—ensures you gain a clearer understanding of where your money is going. This awareness leads to mindful spending, where each purchase is deliberate and aligned with your financial goals. Ever notice how small, habitual expenses add up over time? Skipping that daily latte might seem insignificant at first, but over a year, those savings can contribute to a substantial emergency fund or investment. When people are financially responsible, they're better equipped to contribute positively to their communities and the broader economy. Can you imagine a world where individuals are not drowning in debt but instead thriving due to sound financial practices? The collective result is a more stable and prosperous society.

Final Insights

As we draw this chapter to a close, remember that a well-crafted budget is like the perfect recipe—balancing essential ingredients with a sprinkle of luxury. By distinguishing between essential and nonessential expenses, you create a financial feast that sustains your needs while allowing for occasional treats. Prioritizing rent, groceries, and transportation ensures you're covered on all fronts, avoiding those nasty surprise shortages that can leave you scrambling. We've also discussed how different budgeting methods—like the 50/30/20 rule, zero-based budgeting, and the envelope system—can suit various lifestyles, helping you to keep every dollar accountable.

But even the most delicious budget allows for dessert! Allocating funds for nonessentials like dining out or entertainment won't break the bank if done wisely. The key lies in maintaining a flexible approach, adjusting as needed when unexpected costs pop up. Keep tracking your spending habits with tools and templates, ensuring you're always one step ahead. This balance between meeting needs and enjoying wants leads to a fulfilling financial journey, making budgeting less about deprivation and more about wise choices.

Just as every artist needs the right brush to bring their vision to life, the tools you choose can shape your financial masterpiece. In the next chapter, we'll explore a range of budgeting tools and techniques, both digital and manual, designed to help you create a budget that fits your unique needs and lifestyle like a tailor-made suit.

CHAPTER 5

TOOLS AND TECHNIQUES FOR BUDGETING

Creating and maintaining an effective budget is like training for a marathon—it takes the right gear, a solid plan, and steady discipline. With both digital and manual tools at your disposal, you can build endurance and turn your financial habits into a smooth, well-paced stride. And let's be honest: While it may never be as fun as binge-watching your favorite Netflix series, mastering your money can give you the freedom to enjoy those little luxuries without guilt.

Popular Budgeting Apps and Software

If you've ever felt like budgeting is about as fun as a trip to the dentist, you're not alone. Here's the good news: Digital tools have come to the rescue, promising to transform your financial chaos into a symphony of organization with minimal effort from your side.

First up, let's talk about the MVPs of the budgeting app world: Snoop, Quicken Simplifi, YNAB (You Need a Budget), and PocketGuard. Each of these apps brings something unique to the table.

Snoop

Snoop shines by being more than just a number-cruncher. It's like having a financial detective on your side, sniffing out hidden savings, hunting for better deals on your bills, and alerting you to any quirky transactions. With Snoop's personalized tips, you'll get savvy recommendations that make saving money feel like a breeze and keep your budget on point. The Snoop app offers both free and paid subscription options. The basic version is free to use, allowing you to track spending, set budgets, and connect multiple bank accounts. However, they also offer a premium version called *Snoop Plus*, which includes additional features such as unlimited custom spending categories and reports. (Snoop Money-Saving App, n.d.).

Quicken Simplifi

Quicken Simplifi stands out for its simplicity and personalization. It automatically categorizes transactions, adapts to your spending habits, and offers real-time financial insights. The app's intuitive design makes it easy to create custom budgets and track goals, ensuring a stress-free money management experience. Quicken Simplifi requires a paid subscription; however, it also offers a 30-day free trial (*Quicken Simplifi*, n.d.).

YNAB (You Need a Budget)

YNAB is like the boot camp instructor you never knew you needed, but trust me, you do. It adheres to a zero-based budgeting system, which means that every dollar you earn has a job—whether it's paying rent, buying groceries, or taking care of that Netflix subscription you can't live without. YNAB offers monthly and annual subscription plans, but they also have a 34-day free trial (Holzhauer, 2021).

PocketGuard

PocketGuard is the laid-back, minimalist friend who keeps things simple and straightforward. Its strength lies in showing you how much you've got left to spend after accounting for necessities, bills, and goals, so you don't accidentally blow your budget on those tempting sales. PocketGuard offers both free and paid versions. The free version provides essential budgeting tools, such as tracking spending and setting a single savings goal. However, to access advanced features like unlimited savings goals, customized categories, and detailed spending reports, you will need PocketGuard Plus.

How to Select a Budgeting App

Now that we've met our digital budgeting A-listers, how do you pick the right one? It's essential to choose a budgeting app that aligns with your personal financial goals because, let's face it, no one knows your money habits better than you do. Begin by identifying what you need most from a budgeting tool. Are you looking for detailed, hands-on management or something more automated and effortless? If you prefer having control over every penny, Snoop or YNAB might be your best bets. On the other hand, if you want your budgeting efforts to feel almost invisible, Mint or PocketGuard could be ideal.

User reviews can also be highly informative. Real-world experiences shared by other users highlight both the strengths and weaknesses of an app, giving you a sneak peek into any potential pitfalls. And finally, don't forget about cost. While many apps offer free versions, the premium options do come with monthly or annual fees. Make sure the features offered are worth the investment (Holzhauer, 2021).

Linking Accounts to Streamline Budgeting

Once you've selected your app, linking your accounts can save you heaps of time and stress. You don't have to worry about manually entering each transaction (unless you're a fan of self-inflicted tedium). Automated syncing allows your app to track your income and expenses in real time, providing you with up-to-date information about your finances at the touch of a button. This streamlines your budgeting process and enhances accuracy. After all, human error happens, even to the best of us.

Linking accounts is particularly beneficial if you have multiple streams of income or various expenses spread across different platforms. Whether it's your paycheck, freelance earnings, or even passive income from investments, having everything in one place simplifies oversight and helps you maintain a cohesive budget. Many apps, like Goodbudget, tout their manual entry systems, which can be surprisingly effective for those who want to exercise extreme control over their finances. However, the ability to link accounts directly can be a game-changer for convenience and accuracy (McMullen, 2024).

Pro Tips for Keeping Budgeting Apps

But wait, your newfound budgeting bliss doesn't end there! To truly leverage the power of these apps, you need to keep them updated. Regularly reviewing the app's features ensures you're utilizing them fully. Apps frequently roll out new functionalities and shortcuts designed to improve user experience and efficiency. Missing out on these updates is like still using a rotary phone when everyone else has moved on to smartphones. Staying engaged with user support and forums also provides continuous learning opportunities. These communities are often treasure troves of tips and tricks shared by people who have been navigating the same financial waters as you.

Engaging with community resources can also provide motivation and inspiration. Seeing how others achieve their financial goals can prompt you to take advantage of features you haven't yet explored. By setting realistic, achievable financial goals within the app, you're more likely to stay motivated and stick to your plan. It's like having a cheerleader in your pocket, celebrating your small wins and encouraging you to push further. Also, don't shy away from checking out the tutorials and guides many apps offer. These resources can deepen your understanding of budgeting principles and help you get the most out of the app.

The Envelope System for Hands-On Money Management

The envelope system is one of the most old-school yet effective budgeting methods out there. This low-tech approach can be your best friend when it comes to keeping your finances in check, even if you feel like a financial mess. And don't worry, it's pretty straightforward (Grieve, n.d.).

Divide each of your spending categories—for example, groceries, entertainment, and transportation—into envelopes. Instead of swiping a card willy-nilly every time you buy something, you fill these envelopes with actual cash. This means you can't spend more than what's in each envelope. Simple, right? This method isn't just for people who hate math; it's also for those who want to see where their money goes and physically limit overspending.

Now, you might wonder how to adapt this system to suit your financial situation. Start by listing your spending categories. These should cover all your essential needs and a few wants because, hey, we're human. Common categories include groceries, utilities, fun stuff (like that latte you can't live without), and transportation. Once you've identified these, review your past spending. Look at your bank statements or digital receipts to get a realistic idea of how much you spend in each category. Next, decide on an amount to allocate to each envelope based on this history. You can always adjust these amounts as you get the hang of the system. Did you over-allocate for fun stuff but under-budget for groceries? Adjust as needed. Flexibility is key here!

One important approach is to set specific spending limits for each envelope. This will encourage discipline and keep you from splurging. As tempting as it may be to borrow from the fun stuff envelope to fund an unexpected craving for sushi, resist! Only move funds between envelopes in cases of genuine necessity.

Visual cues can be super helpful too. Color-coding your envelopes by category can make things easier to track:

- blue for groceries

- red for bills

- green for saving up for that dream vacation

Another good practice is to regularly review and adjust your envelope allocations. Life happens, expenses change, and your budget should reflect that. Maybe you picked up a new hobby that requires gear, or your utility bills have unexpectedly gone up—revisit and recalibrate your envelopes accordingly.

Now, while the envelope system thrives on its tactile nature, merging it with digital tools can add an extra layer of convenience and insight. Think of it as combining the best of both worlds. Use budgeting apps to track how much is left in each envelope digitally. Apps like Mvelopes or Goodbudget allow you to set up virtual envelopes that mirror your physical ones (Grieve, n.d.). These apps can send you alerts when you're close to hitting your limits, making sure you don't overspend. Plus, they offer real-time updates on your spending habits, providing a comprehensive overview of where your money is going.

If you're not one for frequent trips to the ATM, you can still make the envelope system work by taking advantage of multiple bank accounts or sub-accounts offered by various online banking platforms in your area. This way, you can still shuffle your money around without dealing with physical cash. When you spend, simply transfer funds from the appropriate digital envelope. It's the same concept, minus the paper cuts.

For instance, if you're budgeting $500 a month for groceries, each time you head to the supermarket, dip into that grocery envelope. If by mid-month you notice you're already running low, it's time to reconsider that impulse-buy premium ice cream. This visual control provides clarity and keeps temptations in check. But suppose you need emergency car repairs, and your transportation envelope is depleted. With digital tracking, moving funds from another envelope becomes seamless and instantly recorded, ensuring you can address emergencies without derailing your entire budget.

Don't forget the importance of reviewing your budget regularly. Sit down at the end of each month and assess how you did. Did you stick to your limits? Were there any surprise expenses? Could certain categories use more or less funding? This review phase is paramount. It helps you refine your budgeting skills and ensures your envelopes are realistic and supportive of your financial health. Over the long haul, you'll find the balance that works for you, and any surplus left in the envelopes can be rolled over or saved, giving you a nice cushion for future unexpected expenses.

Pro Tips for Maintaining Discipline and Consistency

When it comes to budgeting, sticking to a plan can feel like trying to keep a New Year's resolution past January 2nd. Here are some practical strategies to help you stay committed to your budgeting plans and achieve financial stability, all while keeping a sense of humor about the whole ordeal.

Sharing Your Financial Goals with Friends

Establishing a support system not only helps motivate you but also makes the journey less lonely. Start by announcing your goal to save for a vacation to your best friend. Now, every time you reach for that extra-large latte, they'll remind you that's one step further from sipping margaritas on the beach. Regular check-ins can promote honesty about financial struggles and successes, encouraging mutual growth and understanding. Plus, it's always fun to celebrate those small victories with someone, even if it's just affording fancy cheese once in a while.

Establishing Achievable Budgeting Targets

Goals should be specific, measurable, attainable, relevant, and time-bound (SMART). Avoid aiming for a magical budget that will fix all life's woes overnight. Instead, set realistic goals. For instance, save $500 in three months rather than $10,000 by next week. Celebrate small milestones along the way to maintain motivation. Saving enough to buy that book you've been eyeing? Treat yourself! The key here is to ensure your goals resonate personally and are realistically manageable so you don't set yourself up for failure.

Focus on progress rather than striving for an unattainable flawless budget. No one likes a perfectionist—especially in budgeting. Recognize that setbacks are part of the process. Life happens; sometimes, you need that emergency taco run. By accepting that mishaps will occur, you'll maintain a positive outlook on budgeting. Be willing to adapt and modify plans as circumstances change; this develops long-term commitment. The journey to financial stability is gradual and evolves over time. So, give yourself a break when you slip up, and get right back on track.

Employ technology to maintain focus on your budgeting goals. If you can set 28 reminders for your dog's birthday, you can certainly set up notifications for budget reviews. Use apps and digital tools to streamline your tracking efforts. Tools like the ones mentioned earlier, or even simple calendar alerts, can help you stay on top of your finances. Setting reminders for important expenses helps avoid last-minute spending traps that disrupt budgets. What's more, real-time tracking tools reinforce self-awareness around financial habits. Getting an alert that tells you "You've hit your coffee budget" is like having a financially savvy conscience on your phone.

Final Insights

As we've navigated the chaotic sea of budgeting, we've encountered some digital lifeboats like Snoop, Quicken Simplifi, YNAB, and PocketGuard. These apps promise to simplify our financial woes with a few taps and swipes, almost making it fun—like a game where the prize is keeping your money. Whether you're a control freak wanting to micromanage every cent with YNAB or a laid-back spender opting for Quicken Simplifi's effortless simplicity, there's something for everyone. And don't forget, you can always go old-school with the envelope system, reliving the thrill of handling actual cash while pretending you're in a spy movie smuggling secret funds.

In the end, the goal is not to become a budgeting ChatGPT but to find a system that syncs with your lifestyle without driving you bonkers. It's all about balance—combining rigorous tracking with occasional indulgence, whether that's a fancy cheese or an emergency pizza run. Keep adjusting, stay engaged with those handy tutorials, and never stop learning from both digital communities and your own financial mishaps. With the right mix of tools, managing your money can transform from a dreaded chore into a surprisingly rewarding activity (yes, seriously).

Much like a gardener tends to their plants to ensure they flourish, regularly monitoring and adjusting your budget is key to nurturing your financial health. In the next chapter, we'll explore how to keep your budget in bloom by consistently reviewing and revising it, ensuring you stay aligned with your goals and adapt to any changes along the way.

CHAPTER 6

MONITORING AND ADJUSTING YOUR BUDGET

Regularly reviewing and revising your budget is like giving your finances a bimonthly dental check-up. Sure, it might not be thrilling or Instagram-worthy, but it prevents cavities of debt from ruining your financial smile. It's far too easy to get lost in the whirlwind of daily expenses without noticing where all your hard-earned bucks are sneaking off to. Before you know it, those little expenditures—an extra coffee here, an off-the-cuff sale purchase there—add up faster than canned laughter on a sitcom. The key is to keep tabs on your spending habits consistently, so you're steering your financial vehicle with purpose rather than swerving frantically when the potholes of overdraft fees appear on the road.

The Importance of Monthly Budget Check-ins

Conducting regular reviews of your budget is like checking the oil in your car—a simple routine task that can save you from major headaches down the road. It's easy to get caught up in the daily grind and forget to look at the bigger picture of your finances. However, taking the time to do so monthly can make a world of difference when it comes to achieving your long-term financial goals (Batch, 2024).

Monthly check-ins are the unsung heroes of personal finance. Sure, they might seem tedious, but think of them as the GPS for your money. Without these regular reviews, you're navigating blindfolded, hoping you don't crash into a mountain of debt. By closely examining your income and expenditures each month, you'll have a clearer picture of your financial landscape. This practice helps you understand where your money is coming from and, more importantly, where it's going.

Heaven forbid, but let's say you discover that you're spending $50 a week on lattes. That's $200 a month or $2,400 a year just fueling your caffeine habit. With a little insight, you might decide to cut down or find a cheaper alternative, freeing up funds for more critical financial goals. Reviewing your budget regularly sharpens your understanding and keeps you financially literate, helping you avoid surprising costs and track your financial health accurately.

Speaking of surprises, who likes those unexpected expenses that pop up like uninvited party crashers? Regularly reviewing your budget allows for necessary adjustments based on changes in income or expenses. Did your electric bill skyrocket because your kid suddenly decided that their bedroom must be kept at arctic temperatures? Or did you finally get that well-deserved raise at work? Monthly reviews enable you to tweak your budget accordingly to avoid nasty surprises. When something in your financial life changes, your budget should change too. An ounce of prevention is worth a pound of cure, as the old saying goes, and nowhere is this truer than in budgeting.

Beyond preventing surprises, regular reviews give you valuable insights into your spending trends. This is your chance to channel your inner Hercule Poirot and uncover areas of overspending. Maybe one category in your budget is consistently higher than expected. Identifying these patterns empowers you to make informed decisions about where to cut back. Do you really need three streaming service subscriptions when you only binge-watch one show at a time? Recognizing these habits can lead to more mindful spending and better allocation of your resources across the Orient Express.

Scheduled reviews help reduce feelings of overwhelm. Let's face it, finances can be intimidating, and many people shy away from looking at their bank statements simply out of fear. But guess what? Acting like an ostrich and sticking your head in the ground doesn't make it go away; it just makes it scarier. By setting aside a specific time each month to review your finances, you break down the massive, looming beast of "money management" into smaller, manageable chunks. It's like transforming a financial monster into a friendly hamster, still needing care and attention but not nearly as threatening. If you want to feel more secure and focused on your financial goals, making these reviews a part of your routine will go a long way.

So, how do you set this up without feeling like you've been sentenced to financial jail? Keep it simple. Choose a day each month, like the first Sunday, and mark it on your calendar as financial review day. Grab a cup of your favorite beverage and sit down with your latest bank statements. Look at your income first. Is it steady? Did you get any bonuses or extra earnings? Next, tackle your expenditures. Don't just skim them but go through item by item. Highlight anything that stands out or feels excessive. Make notes of any upcoming expenses you didn't account for last month, like medical bills or annual insurance payments.

Now, here's the part many people skip but I promise is worth it: Reflect on what you've learned from your review. Did you manage to save more than planned? High-five yourself! Did you overspend in an area? No worries; identify why that happened and plan to adjust next month. The beauty of monthly reviews is that they're short enough to notice problems early and frequent enough to address them before they spiral out of control.

When you conduct these monthly check-ins, you're not just managing money; you're enhancing your financial literacy. Regularly familiarizing yourself with your budget means you're learning continuously. Consequently, you become more adept at spotting issues and finding solutions. Financial wellness is a marathon, not a sprint. Think of these reviews as your training regimen, building your strength and endurance over time.

Pro Tips for Managing Months When Money Is Tight

When the going gets tough financially, it's easy to feel like you're stuck in a never-ending game of "Budget Jenga," where one wrong move might cause everything to come crashing down. Nonetheless, many practical strategies can help you weather the storm during those less-than-pleasant months.

First and foremost, focus on prioritizing essential expenses by creating a hierarchy of spending based on immediate needs. You're like a strict traffic cop, directing your cash flow to the most critical areas: housing, utilities, groceries, and transportation. Everything else can wait at the red light until your essentials get the green signal. Paying rent or mortgage should always take precedence over that tantalizing impulse buy you've been eyeing. Without a stable roof over your head, even the best meal-prepping skills won't prevent you from personal finance purgatory.

Consider short-term solutions such as altering payment timelines or negotiating bills to alleviate financial pressure. Think of it as playing a high-stakes game of "Financial Tetris." You can call service providers and ask for extended deadlines or payment plans, which can help fit those larger expenses into your current financial puzzle without causing too much pandemonium. This temporary adjustment can provide some breathing room, allowing you to tackle other pressing financial matters. Have you ever tried convincing your internet provider to give you a break? Surprisingly, they sometimes do! And if they don't budge, well, switching to a cheaper plan could be another strategic move.

You should embrace frugality through smart shopping, meal planning, and cutting back on nonessential retail indulgences. Scout out sales, discounts, and coupons like a bloodhound on a scent trail. Meal planning is another cornerstone of frugality. By organizing your meals for the week, you can dodge the temptation of expensive takeout and avoid letting random ingredients wither away in the depths of your fridge. An added bonus: You'll end up with fewer science experiments growing in forgotten corners.

Maintaining a positive mindset is crucial. View budgeting as a tool for empowerment, not restriction. You're the captain of your own financial ship, plotting a course towards financial freedom with every wise move.

Recognizing and Rewarding Your Budgeting Successes

Celebrating budgeting wins might seem like an excuse to splurge, but, believe it or not, it's a savvy move that keeps the financial gears well-oiled and running smoothly. Let's explore why giving yourself a pat on the back for good budgeting is not just fluff but a solid strategy to stay motivated and on track (FAIRWINDS, 2023).

Keeping a record of your achievements is more than just collecting gold stars in your financial diary. It serves as tangible proof that all those sacrifices you made actually lead somewhere. So, you've been diligently sticking to your budget for months now. At first, it might feel like you're trudging through mud, cutting spa days here, skipping out on pricey dinners there. But when you have a visible record of these victories, it shines as a constant reminder of your progress. Whether it's a neatly maintained journal, a digital tracker, or a simple spreadsheet brimming with green ticks, each entry is a nod to your hard work and discipline. "Hey look, I saved $500 this month by skipping my daily Burger King run!" This isn't just a number; it's a badge of honor that speaks volumes about your commitment to financial wellness.

What's more, establishing a reward system doesn't mean you blow half your savings on a luxury cruise because, yay, you managed to save some dough! The idea here is to set up simple, budget-friendly rewards that encourage you to keep at it. When you hit your monthly savings goal, treat yourself to a movie night at home with all the frills: popcorn, soda, the works. What about that shoe you've been eyeing for weeks? Go ahead, it's yours, guilt-free! These small rewards create a positive reinforcement loop, making budgeting less of a chore and more of a game where you're constantly earning points (and prizes) for playing smart.

Sharing your successes is another powerful motivator. You know how everyone loves a good underdog story? Well, think of yourself as the Denzel or Meryl in your own budgeting Hollywood saga. Sharing your wins with friends or a community can offer that much-needed boost to stay on track. When you share that you finally paid off a nagging credit card debt, you're not just patting yourself on the back—you're also inspiring others around you to follow suit. Having a supportive peer group means you've got people cheering you on, providing that extra push when the going gets tough. It turns what could be a solitary, daunting task into a collective effort where every win is celebrated together. Plus, nothing beats a well-timed high-five from a friend who's genuinely happy for your progress!

Taking time to reflect on your achievements cannot be overstated in refining future goals. It's essential to occasionally step back and review the journey so far. What did you do right? Where could you improve? Maybe you excelled at cutting down unnecessary luxury bath products or premium snacks, but struggled with controlling impulse buys. Reflecting on these points helps in fine-tuning your budgeting strategies moving forward. Understanding your strengths allows you to set more realistic and achievable goals while learning from your weaknesses lets you anticipate challenges better. Let's say you notice that you saved more during the months when you budgeted for social outings rather than the months when you tried avoiding them altogether. Then, you might adjust your future budgets to include these small indulgences in a controlled manner. Not only does this keep you balanced, but it also makes sticking to the budget a lot more sustainable in the long run.

So go ahead, celebrate those wins—big or small. Your wallet will thank you, and your motivation will skyrocket, proving that even the smallest victory deserves its 15 minutes of fame. Keep tracking your progress, reward yourself wisely, share your successes, and never stop refining your goals. It's not just about where you end up but also about how you get there. Here's to making budgeting as enjoyable as possible, one small victory at a time!

Final Insights

So, if you want to avoid financial potholes, keep those budget reviews rolling every month. Think of it like a monthly money check-up, keeping you fit and ready to tackle any surprising expenses that might spring up like an overly enthusiastic pop quiz. We've navigated the waters of splurge habits, unpredictable utility bills, and frivolous expenditures with the trusty compass of our budget review. By making these monthly check-ins a habit, you're not just steering clear of financial chaos but also becoming a savvy detective, spotting spending patterns before they turn into trouble.

In essence, regular budget reviews are key. They save you from unexpected shocks and help you stay on course toward your goals. By keeping tabs on where your money goes and making adjustments as needed, you transform an intimidating task into a manageable routine. Remember, this isn't about turning your life into a no-fun zone; it's about ensuring your finances support your dreams and aspirations. So, mark your calendar, and dig into those numbers. Your future self will thank you!

Thinking of how ol' Vinny tunes up his car to ensure it has a *Fast and Furious* performance, the next chapter will help you fine-tune your earning potential. We'll explore ways to boost your income through career development, side hustles, and passive income opportunities, providing you with the tools to drive your financial success forward.

UNIT 2: RESOURCES AND TOOLS

Budgeting apps:

- PocketGuard

- Mvelopes

- Quicken Simplifi

Emergency fund tools:

- Acorns

- Qapital

- Digit

- Chime

UNIT 3: MAXIMIZING YOUR INCOME

CHAPTER 7

ENHANCING YOUR EARNING POTENTIAL

Maximizing your earnings is a bit like navigating a maze in a storm—exhilarating with every twist and turn but daunting as you strive to stay on the right path. Whether you're thinking about climbing the career ladder, dabbling in side hustles, or dreaming of that sweet, sweet passive income, there's a lot to consider. This isn't about searching for spare change or cutting corners. Instead, it's about spotting real opportunities to grow your wealth without ending up in a straitjacket.

Identifying Pathways for Career Advancement

Finding ways to advance your career isn't just about moving up the ranks; it involves understanding your abilities and discovering the right paths that fit your goals and passions (Career Development and Employee Satisfaction, 2024).

Understanding Your Value

The only way to do great work is to love what you do. So, recognizing your unique skills, lets you truly comprehend your value. It's like being at a potluck dinner, and everyone brings something different to the table. Each of us has distinct talents and abilities that we bring to our jobs. Identifying these skills can help you stand out and position yourself for greater opportunities.

To do this, start by reflecting on what makes you unique. Maybe it's your knack for problem-solving or your ability to stay calm under pressure. Write down your strengths and keep an eye out for moments when these qualities shine through in your work. Feedback from colleagues and supervisors can also be a goldmine. Don't hesitate to ask for constructive criticism; it can offer insights into areas where you excel and those that need some polishing.

Knowing your worth isn't just about feeling good—it allows you to leverage this knowledge to enhance your career. If you are aware of your strengths, you can better advocate for yourself during performance reviews and interviews. Highlighting your unique skills can make you an invaluable asset to your team, leading to potential raises and promotions.

Seeking Professional Development

Engaging in continuous learning through upskilling, certifications, and courses is another effective way to maximize your earnings. Think of it as upgrading your phone's software—you get enhanced features, improved performance, and sometimes even a new look. The same goes for your career. Continuous learning keeps you competitive and opens doors to new opportunities.

Start by identifying the skills that are in high demand in your industry. Websites like LinkedIn Learning, Coursera, and Udemy offer a plethora of courses that can help you acquire these skills. Sometimes, your employer might even sponsor these courses, so it's worth bringing it up with your manager.

Certifications can also add significant value to your resume. Project management certifications like PMP can make you a more attractive candidate for leadership roles. Tech professionals can benefit from acquiring certifications in programming languages or cybersecurity, as well as gaining expertise in emerging fields like artificial intelligence (AI) or machine learning (ML).

Don't underestimate the power of workshops and seminars either. These events offer not only educational benefits but also networking opportunities. You can learn a lot from industry leaders and fellow attendees, gaining insights that can propel your career forward.

Building Your Network

Actively nurturing professional relationships can provide unmatched job insights and opportunities. Remember the old saying, "It's not what you know, but who you know"? While skills and knowledge are undeniably important, having a strong network can significantly boost your career prospects.

One way to build your network is by participating in industry events such as conferences, webinars, and trade shows. These settings offer a relaxed environment for meeting people who share your professional interests. Don't be shy about introducing yourself and exchanging contact information. A simple follow-up email after the event can go a long way in establishing a meaningful connection.

Social platforms like LinkedIn, X (formally known as Twitter), and GitHub are also powerful tools for networking. Keep your profile updated and actively engage with posts related to your field. Join relevant groups and participate in discussions to increase your visibility. The more you interact, the more likely it is that you'll attract attention from industry professionals and recruiters.

Another valuable strategy is mentorship, both giving and receiving. Finding a mentor can provide guidance and open doors you didn't even know existed. On the flip side, mentoring others can solidify your own knowledge and broaden your network. Mentorship creates a mutually beneficial relationship that can lead to growth and new opportunities.

Setting Career Goals

Defining clear, specific, measurable career goals is essential for staying aligned with your professional ambitions. Think of it as setting your Google Maps before setting out on a road trip. Without a destination in mind, you could end up anywhere—or nowhere.

Start by identifying your long-term career aspirations. What role do you see yourself in five or ten years down the line? Break this big picture down into smaller, manageable milestones. If you aim to become a department head, intermediate steps might include gaining experience in different roles within the department, acquiring relevant certifications, and building leadership skills.

Once you've set your goals, it's vital to track your progress. Create a timeline and set deadlines for each milestone. Regularly revisit these goals to evaluate how far you've come and adjust them as needed. This approach ensures you remain on track and allows you to celebrate small victories along the way, keeping you motivated.

The road to success is always under construction. Share your objectives with a trusted colleague or mentor who can offer encouragement and guidance. Regular check-ins can help you stay focused and committed to your path.

Finding Side Gigs That Fit Your Skills and Interests

Identifying and pursuing side gigs that complement your skills and passions can be a great way to boost your income without sacrificing your main job. The key is to make sure these side hustles are aligned with what you enjoy and are good at, which makes the extra work feel less like a chore and more like an extension of your personal interests.

For starters, evaluate what skills you can monetize outside of your primary job. Begin by listing all your talents and hobbies, no matter how small they might seem. Are you good at graphic design? Do you enjoy writing or tutoring? Maybe you have a knack for fixing gadgets or providing excellent customer service. Once you have this list, think about which of these skills have received compliments or praise from others. Have people turned to you for help in these areas? Do you see others making money from similar skills? Asking these questions can help you identify your marketable skills (Wilson, 2020).

Then, explore online platforms like:

- Freelancer

- FlexJobs

- Toptal

- Behance

- Dribbble

- Upwork

- Fiverr

- Etsy

These provide countless opportunities to turn your talents into paying gigs. These digital marketplaces have a wide range of categories, so you're likely to find something that fits your specific abilities. For local opportunities, networking with nearby businesses can also open doors. Small business owners often look for freelancers to handle tasks that don't require a full-time employee, such as social media management, content creation, or website development.

Managing a side hustle effectively alongside your main job requires setting clear boundaries. Allocate specific hours during the week dedicated solely to your side hustle. This might mean working in the evenings or using part of your weekend, but it's important to stick to this schedule to avoid burnout. Prioritize deadlines and learn to say no when necessary. If you take on too much, both your main job and your side gig can suffer. Great time-management is like a well-tended garden, both yielding the best results when nurtured consistently.

Once you've landed some gigs, maximizing your earning potential involves several strategies. Firstly, price your services competitively. Research what others in your field are charging and position yourself accordingly. Offering slightly lower rates initially can help you attract clients and build a portfolio. As you gain positive reviews and repeat business, you can gradually increase your prices.

Upselling is another effective tactic. It's like offering someone a second slice of pizza after they've already polished off the first—it's hard to resist when they're already hooked! If you offer basic graphic design services, for example, consider adding premium options like logo creation, branding packages, or expedited delivery for an additional fee. Building a solid portfolio showcasing your best work can also make a significant difference. Potential clients want to see evidence of your capabilities, so keep your portfolio updated with recent projects and any glowing reviews from previous clients.

Understanding Passive Income Sources

Passive income is a financial buzzword many aspire to include in their personal finance strategy, but what does it really mean? In simple terms, passive income refers to earnings derived from sources other than your active efforts. Unlike wages or salary—which require you to be physically present and perform tasks to get paid—passive income sources keep the money coming even when you're asleep, sipping coffee, or enjoying a beach vacation. It's your way of having the money work for you instead of you working for money.

The concept might sound like a dream, but it's essential to differentiate passive income from active income. Active income involves consistent, direct efforts, such as your day job, freelance projects, or any work where you have to "show up" either physically or mentally. On the other hand, passive income requires an initial investment of time, effort, or money but demands minimal to no ongoing effort afterward. The beauty of passive income is like having a money tree in your backyard; it keeps growing and providing financial security and freedom, letting you achieve long-term goals without stressing over day-to-day expenses.

Exploring Investment Options

When it comes to passive income, there a few methods that are highly promising (Royal, 2024):

- **Real estate investment:** By purchasing rental properties, you can earn a steady stream of income through rent payments. Real estate can appreciate in value over time, adding to your asset base.

However, managing properties can sometimes morph into more active involvement if you opt not to hire property managers.

- **Dividend-paying stocks:** Investing in stocks that pay dividends gives you periodic payments based on the company's profits. This method allows you to benefit from the growth of the stock market, providing both capital appreciation and regular income. Start by researching companies with a strong track record of dividend payments to ensure a stable revenue stream.

- **Peer-to-peer lending platforms:** These platforms connect borrowers with investors willing to fund loans in exchange for interest payments. Though riskier than investing in established stocks or real estate, peer-to-peer lending offers higher returns and diversifies your investment portfolio. It's like being a mini-banker but without the stuffy office and dress code.

Creating Digital Products

In today's digital age, creating digital products such as e-books or online courses or crafting affiliate marketing websites can become robust passive income streams. Once the initial setup is complete, these digital assets can generate revenue with minimal ongoing effort (Royal, 2024).

- **E-books:** Writing an e-book on a topic you're passionate about or knowledgeable in can help you tap into the vast online marketplace of readers hungry for information. Selling your e-book on platforms like Amazon Kindle Direct Publishing, Lulu, IngramSpark, and Smashwords ensures that once published, sales and distribution are automated.

- **Online course development:** Developing online courses can turn your expertise into a goldmine. Platforms like Udemy, Teachable, and

Skillshare allow you to create comprehensive courses in areas ranging from cooking to coding. The key here is to invest time in making a quality course, complete with clear instructions, engaging content, and supportive resources. Once done, these courses can sell repeatedly without requiring further input from you.

- **Affiliate marketing:** Promoting other people's products through blogs or social media channels allows you to earn a commission on each sale made via your referral link. This model thrives on the principle of generating traffic to your affiliate links and ensuring a steady stream of visitors to your site or social media profile. You could review products, write how-to guides, or create listicles that entice clicks on your affiliate links.

Pro Tips for Automating Income Streams

To maximize the time you save and minimize the effort required, automation becomes a game-changer in maintaining passive income. Technology today lets you automate your income streams like having a robotic butler—while you kick back and relax, it's busy keeping everything running smoothly with minimal oversight (5 Simple Automated Business Ideas, 2024).

- **Automated payments and reminders:** Setting up automatic payments and reminders for your rental properties ensures timely collection and fewer headaches. Property management software can handle everything from lease agreements to maintenance requests, freeing you up from being on constant landlord duty.

- **Automate commission:** Websites and blogs that generate ad revenue or affiliate commissions can also be automated. Tools like WordPress plugins can schedule posts, optimize your website's performance, and update your content regularly. Email marketing software helps maintain seamless communication with your audience, sending out newsletters or promotional emails automatically based on user behavior or set schedules.

- **Automate sales and tracking:** Online platforms for selling digital products, such as Teachable for courses or Etsy for handmade crafts, offer built-in features for sales automation, inventory tracking, and customer relationship management. This self-sustaining mechanism allows your initial hard work to continue paying off without manual intervention.

- **Automate financial investments:** Robo-advisors like Betterment or Wealthfront offer automated investment services, managing your portfolio based on defined parameters such as risk tolerance and financial goals. They rebalance your portfolio periodically and reinvest dividends, ensuring optimal performance without requiring you to constantly monitor the stock market.

Final Insights

In this chapter, we've wandered through the intriguing world of career upgrades, side gigs, and passive income like explorers on a treasure hunt. We've dug up the golden nuggets that can help you recognize your unique skills and leverage them for career advancement. When you continue learning and growing professionally, you'll see how updating your skill set is much like upgrading your phone's software, leading to better performance and exciting new features in your career. You've also dipped your toes into the networking pool, appreciating the value of mentorship and professional relationships. Setting clear career goals was likened to entering coordinates into Google Maps, ensuring you stay on target and celebrate milestones along the way.

But we didn't stop there; side hustles entered the scene like uninvited guests who actually end up being the life of the party. We explored how finding gigs that match your hobbies and skills can make extra work feel less like drudgery and more like passion projects. Then, we took a tranquil stroll into the realm of passive income. Who knew making money while sipping coffee could be an actual thing? Whether it's real estate investments, dividend stocks, or digital products, these income streams promise financial freedom with minimal ongoing effort. And let's not forget the magic of automation, which ensures your efforts continue to pay off without needing constant attention. So, take these strategies to heart, and let's turn those financial dreams into reality!

Now that we've discussed the ins and outs of managing and growing your income, it's time to shift gears and focus on how to make the most of what you earn. Next, we'll uncover strategies to optimize your employee benefits, allocate bonuses wisely, and stretch your income further. These insights will empower you to enhance your financial situation and turn every dollar into a tiny, diligent worker bee, buzzing around to build your financial hive.

Chapter 8

Making the Most of What You Earn

Optimizing employee benefits, allocating bonuses wisely, and stretching your income might seem as exciting as watching grass grow, but trust me, these actions can make a significant difference in your financial health. Imagine having the magical ability to turn "blah" into "ta-da!" by simply making the most of what's already on your plate. We're talking about unraveling the power hidden in your compensation package, which isn't just a pile of formalities thrown at you during onboarding. With a little know-how, those boring-sounding benefits can morph into a treasure trove of opportunities that keep your wallet smiling and your stress levels low.

Understanding and Maximizing Employee Benefits

Employee benefits are like the hidden gems of a compensation package, offering incredible value that often goes unnoticed. When you tap into these resources, you can significantly improve your finances.

Health Insurance Options

Choosing the right health insurance plan can feel like navigating an intricate maze, but the right choice can lead to substantial savings on healthcare costs.

Health insurance typically covers a range of services including hospitalization, prescription drugs, preventive care, and mental health services. When selecting a plan, it's crucial to compare factors such as premiums, deductibles, co-payments, and coverage for dependents. Some companies even offer dental, vision, and alternative medicine coverage. Opt for a plan that aligns with your medical needs and those of your family to avoid paying out-of-pocket for essential services. A comprehensive health insurance plan isn't just a safety net; it serves as a tool for managing your money better by reducing unexpected medical expenses (Cross, 2024).

Retirement Contributions

Employer-sponsored retirement plans are often the bedrock of long-term financial security. These plans allow you to not only save for retirement but also benefit from tax advantages. One of the most critical aspects of these plans is employer matching contributions. Think of it as free money—for every dollar you contribute up to a certain percentage, your employer matches it. This match accelerates your savings without any additional effort on your part. Let's say your employer offers a 100% match up to 5% of your salary; contributing 5% means your employer adds another 5%, effectively doubling your contribution. Always strive to contribute at least enough to get the full employer match because turning down this free money is akin to leaving part of your salary unclaimed (Ossevoort, 2024).

Flexible Spending Accounts (FSAs)

FSAs or similar schemes, depending on where you are based, allow you to set aside pre-tax dollars to cover qualified medical, dental, and vision expenses not covered by insurance. Contributions to an FSA reduce your taxable income, which can result in significant tax savings. The funds in an FSA can be used for various healthcare costs such as co-pays, deductibles, prescription medications, and even some over-the-counter items. However, FSAs generally come with a "use-it-or-lose-it" provision, meaning that any unused funds at the end of the plan year may be forfeited. Therefore, careful planning is essential to maximize the benefits of an FSA without losing contributions. Despite this caveat, schemes like FSAs remain a powerful tool for managing healthcare costs efficiently while lowering your taxable income (Ossevoort, 2024).

Perks and Benefits

Many companies offer lesser-known benefits such as employee discounts, gym memberships, wellness programs, commuter benefits, tuition reimbursement, and employee assistance programs (EAPs)—depending on the country you live and work in. Employee discounts can save you money on everyday purchases, while gym memberships and wellness programs promote physical health and well-being. Commuter benefits can lower the cost of traveling to and from work, making your daily commute more affordable. Tuition reimbursement programs support ongoing education and skill development, potentially leading to higher future income. EAPs or similar programs provide confidential counseling and support services for personal or work-related issues, promoting mental health and emotional well-being. Taking advantage of these additional perks not only enhances your quality of life but also contributes to your overall financial stability (Cross, 2024).

Understanding employee benefits might feel like solving a Rubik's Cube blindfolded, but once you figure it out, you'll unlock a world of opportunities for improving both your finances and your well-being. Let's break down some guidelines to help you effectively leverage these benefits:

- **Evaluate your needs:** Assess your healthcare needs, family requirements, and long-term financial goals. This assessment will guide you in selecting the most appropriate health insurance plan and other benefits.

- **Understand plan details:** Fully understand the specifics of each offered benefit. For health insurance, understand what services are covered and the associated costs. For retirement plans, grasp the employer's matching policy and vesting schedules.

- **Maximize employer contributions:** Always contribute enough to your retirement plan to receive the full employer match. It's essentially free money that boosts your savings.

- **Plan FSA contributions wisely:** Estimate your annual healthcare expenses to determine a suitable FSA contribution amount. Aim to use all the funds within the plan year to avoid forfeiture.

- **Utilize additional perks:** Stay informed about all available employee perks. Enroll in wellness programs, use employee discounts, and explore tuition reimbursement opportunities to make the most of your compensation package.

Smart Ways to Allocate Bonuses and Extra Income

One of the most exhilarating moments in personal finance is receiving a bonus or windfall. It feels like money falling from the sky, ready to be used for anything your heart desires. However, before you rush off to buy that sleek gadget or plan a spontaneous getaway, consider how you can use this extra income to fortify your financial future. Channeling your bonuses wisely can help you build a solid foundation for long-term financial stability. Here are some effective strategies to optimize any bonus or extra income.

Emergency Savings Fund

Life has a knack for surprising us with unexpected expenses, whether it's a medical emergency, a sudden car repair, or even a job loss. That's where an emergency fund comes into play. The goal is to have three to six months' worth of living expenses saved up. Start by setting aside a portion of your bonus toward this fund.

Think of it as your financial cushion, ready to soften the blow of those unplanned misadventures. This strategic move will not only provide peace of mind but also prevent you from accumulating debt when the unexpected occurs (What to Do with Extra Cash, n.d.).

Debt Repayment Strategies

High-interest debts, such as credit card balances, can cripple your finances with their relentless interest charges. Use a significant part of your bonus to pay down these high-interest debts first because let's face it, every dollar paid off is a tiny victory against future interest payments. Prioritizing these obligations ensures you minimize the amount of money you'll fork out in interest over the long run. For example, if you have a $5,000 credit card debt with a 20% interest rate, you'll save hundreds of dollars in interest by paying it off faster. Once that weight is lifted, don't forget to establish a plan to prevent future balances from piling up (What to Do with Extra Cash, n.d.).

Investing in Growth

One of the most profitable investments you can make is in yourself. Using your bonus to further your education or acquire new skills can lead to higher income potentials down the road. Whether it's taking a certification course, attending a workshop, or even pursuing a degree, these investments often yield significant returns. They enhance your marketability while opening doors to career advancements and opportunities that might otherwise remain closed. A friend of mine, for instance, used her bonus to complete a digital marketing course. Within a year, she landed a high-paying job that she previously couldn't qualify for.

Yet, investing isn't limited to personal development alone. Consider putting some funds into retirement accounts available in your country. These accounts offer tax benefits and are vital for long-term financial wellness. Aim to contribute 10–15% of your pre-tax salary each year to your retirement savings. If you're already maxed out on those contributions, explore other investment options like brokerage accounts or automated investing platforms. This ensures that your money continues to work for you, growing and compounding over time (Facet, 2024).

Rewarding Yourself

While focusing on savings and investments is crucial, let's not forget the importance of rewarding yourself. After all, personal finance is also about finding balance and maintaining happiness. Small indulgences can be motivation to stick to your financial plans and avoid burnout. Allocate a small portion of your bonus for activities or items that bring you joy. Maybe it's that cooking class you've always wanted to take, or perhaps it's a weekend trip to recharge your batteries. Remember, moderation is key. By striking the right balance between saving and spending, you maintain enthusiasm for your financial journey without feeling deprived.

Pro Tips for Living Within Your Means

Maintaining a lifestyle that aligns with your income is crucial for achieving financial peace and satisfaction. Here's some actionable advice that can help you live within your means while enjoying a fulfilling life (Frugal Living, 2024).

Creating a Spending Plan

Think of a spending plan as your financial roadmap, helping you navigate every twist and turn of your expenses. Start by listing all sources of income—whether it's from your job, side hustles, or investments. Next, categorize your expenses: rent or mortgage, utilities, groceries, entertainment, etc. This will help you see where your money is going.

- **Guideline:** Break down your expenses into categories and track them over a few months. This will give you an accurate picture of where adjustments might be needed.

Evaluating Expenditures

Once you've categorized your expenditures, it's time to evaluate them. Are there areas where you're spending more than necessary? Perhaps that daily latte run isn't as innocent as it seems. Identifying these "wallet vampires" is the first step toward better financial well-being. For example, if you find you're spending $200 a month on pub crawling, consider setting a limit or finding cheaper alternatives like popping that cold one at home.

- **Guideline:** Set realistic spending limits for each category based on your evaluation. Don't forget to allow some wiggle room for unexpected expenses.

Mindful Consumption

This is all about being intentional with how you spend your money. Instead of making impulsive purchases, take a step back and ask yourself some critical questions: Do I really need this? Will it add value to my life? Can I afford it without compromising my budget?

Let's say you're eyeing that sleek, new gadget. Before you whip out your card, think about its utility. Is it genuinely beneficial or just another shiny object vying for your attention? By reflecting on these questions, you can avoid buyer's remorse and make decisions that align with your long-term goals.

- **Guideline:** Implement a 24-hour rule for nonessential purchases. If after 24 hours you still believe it's worth buying, then go ahead. This helps curb impulse buys.

Scaling Back on Nonessentials

Now, this doesn't mean you have to live a life of austerity. It's about trimming the fat off your budget and focusing on what truly matters. Do you really need to buy a new outfit for every occasion? Maybe sticking to a versatile wardrobe would suffice and save you a decent chunk of change.

To identify nonessential expenses, list all your discretionary spending—these are items beyond necessities like food and housing. Examples include subscription services, gym memberships, and luxury goods. Once identified, ask yourself which of these you can cut back on or eliminate altogether. Even small changes, like using a reusable water bottle instead of buying bottled water can add up over time.

- **Guideline:** Perform a monthly audit of your discretionary expenses to see what can be reduced or removed. This practice ensures that you stay on top of your finances and prevent unnecessary leaks.

Community Engagement

Community engagement can be a wonderful way to stretch your income while building new connections. Sharing resources with friends or neighbors can reduce costs significantly. For example, consider organizing a tool-sharing group where members can borrow rather than buy seldom-used tools. This not only saves everyone money but also strengthens community bonds.

Another idea is to participate in community swap meets or borrowing events. These gatherings are excellent for exchanging items you no longer need for things you do, at no cost. What's more, leveraging social media groups focused on frugal living can offer valuable tips and support from like-minded folks. Who knows, you might find recommendations for local thrift stores or free entertainment options.

Reflect and Adjust Regularly

After implementing these strategies, remember that flexibility is key. Life circumstances change, and so might your financial goals. Periodically review your spending habits and adjust your plan accordingly. When you continuously reflect on your budget, it ensures that it remains effective and relevant to your current situation.

Overcoming Challenges

It's normal to face challenges when adopting a more disciplined approach to spending; after all, even your wallet might grumble a bit when it's on a diet! Social pressures and personal habits can sometimes derail your efforts. However, the goal is continuous improvement, not perfection. Seek support from financial advisors or like-minded individuals if you encounter difficulties. "A journey of a thousand miles begins with a single step," so even small steps forward contribute to your overall progress toward financial stability.

Final Insights

As we wrap up, it's clear that optimizing employee benefits and strategically managing bonuses can be like finding financial treasure. Mastering health insurance, boosting retirement savings, and wisely spending bonuses set you up for long-term success while still letting you splurge on the occasional treat! Sticking to your budget, crafting a smart spending plan, and cutting out extras are essential moves. And don't forget to share resources with your community and celebrate those small victories—they're like little confetti moments in your financial journey. Next up, we'll tackle the art of saving on everyday expenses, with tips that will help you cut costs without cutting out the fun.

CHAPTER 9

SAVING ON EVERYDAY EXPENSES

Saving on daily costs is a bit like fishing—you don't need a fancy rod or a captain's hat. With a sharp eye for bargains, a little patience, and some smart bait like coupons or cashback apps, you can reel in some serious savings without even getting your feet wet. The idea is to turn ordinary shopping or bill-paying tasks into a game where the prize is keeping more of your hard-earned money. As daunting as this may sound, once you get the hang of it, you'll wonder why you didn't start earlier.

Pro Tips for Finding the Best Deals and Discounts

When it comes to saving on daily costs, identifying and accessing the best deals is an essential skill that can help you stretch your budget without sacrificing quality.

Price Comparison Websites

These platforms allow you to compare prices across various retailers, ensuring you snatch the best deal available. They're like your personal shopping assistant, tirelessly scouring the web so you don't ave to. Tools like Google Shopping, ShopMania, and Yahoo Shopping aggregate prices from multiple sellers in seconds. This saves you time and prevents the headache of hopping between different sites to check each individual price. You can effortlessly make a quick comparison and informed decisions about where to spend your money most effectively (Niedt, 2021).

Retailer Newsletters

Many stores offer exclusive discounts and promotions to their email subscribers. While it might seem like just another way for retailers to send you spam, the reality is that these newsletters often contain valuable deals that aren't advertised elsewhere. Flash sales, subscriber-only discounts, and early access to promotions can all land directly in your inbox. So, even if your email box gets a bit cluttered, those savings are worth the occasional cleanup session. Just remember to check these emails regularly so you don't miss out on limited-time offers (Schwahn, 2023).

Coupons and Cashback Apps

Apps like Honey and Rakuten search for applicable coupon codes and automatically apply them at checkout. This means you fill up your cart with essentials and then watch the total drop, thanks to a hidden gem of a discount code unearthed by these digital helpers. What's more, cashback apps give you money back on purchases you were already planning to make. This means double savings, where you benefit from the initial discount and get a percentage of your spending refunded. It feels like finding money you didn't know you had (Schwahn, 2023).

Loyalty Programs

Many retailers offer loyalty cards or points-based systems that reward you for frequent shopping. Whether it's accumulating points for every dollar spent or receiving discounts after hitting certain purchase thresholds, these programs can lead to significant savings over time. Grocery stores often have loyalty cards that provide members-only deals or fuel rewards. Engaging in these programs means you're essentially getting paid to shop. The key here is consistency; the more you use these programs, the more benefits you accrue. However, always be mindful not to let the promise of rewards tempt you into unnecessary purchases (Schwahn, 2023).

Incorporating these strategies into your shopping routine doesn't have to be overwhelming. Start small by using a price comparison website for your next big purchase. Gradually add in newsletters and apps to your arsenal, and before you know it, you'll be navigating the world of deals like a pro. It's all about making these practices second nature, turning what might initially feel like extra steps into effortless habits that keep more money in your pocket.

Pro Tips for Lowering Utility and Energy Bills

Reducing fixed monthly expenses can significantly improve financial stability and provide peace of mind. One practical approach to achieving this goal is enhancing energy efficiency and adopting mindful consumption habits.

Conducting an Energy Audit

This assessment can pinpoint where energy is being wasted in your home, identifying simple fixes that lead to immediate savings. Many electric companies offer free audits, performing a room-by-room examination and reviewing your electricity bills. They provide recommendations that you can follow to reduce your electric bill. If this service isn't available for free, you might qualify for the energy-efficient home improvement credit and recoup costs during tax season. Alternatively, you can perform a DIY home energy audit using online resources from reputable organizations like the US Department of Energy. The insights gained from an energy audit are invaluable in reducing unnecessary energy consumption and lowering your monthly utility bills (Grobler, 2024).

Implementing Smart Thermostats and Smart Meters

These devices allow you to program your home's temperature based on your schedule, ensuring that energy isn't used when it's not needed. According to the Department of Energy, adjusting your thermostat by 7°F to 10°F (3.89°C to 5°C) for eight hours a day can save as much as 10% on heating and cooling costs (Grobler, 2024). For instance, during summer, setting the thermostat a bit warmer while you're asleep or away from home can make a notable difference in energy usage. Smart thermostats make it easy to implement these changes by allowing pre-programmed adjustments, ensuring you don't have to remember to do it manually every day. This small investment can lead to significant long-term savings.

Making Minor Behavioral Adjustments

Simple actions like turning off lights when leaving a room or unplugging devices that aren't in use might seem negligible, but they add up over time. Educating household members about the importance of these small changes can create a culture of mindful energy use. For example, unplugging phone chargers or switching off power strips when electronics are not in use prevents vampire energy loss. Cooking with energy-saving appliances, such as slow cookers or pressure cookers, can also save money compared to traditional ovens and stove tops. Plus, washing clothes in cold water and air-drying them instead of using a dryer can lead to lower utility bills. Adopting such habits reduces costs and promotes a more sustainable lifestyle (Grobler, 2024).

Comparing Utility Providers Regularly

Just like shopping for the best deals on products, you should periodically review the rates and services offered by different utility companies. Many people stick with the same provider for years without realizing they could be paying less elsewhere. Comparing rates and consumption patterns ensures you find better deals that suit your needs. Don't hesitate to negotiate with your current provider by presenting them with offers from competitors. Often, companies are willing to match or even beat rival prices to retain customers. Regularly evaluating these options ensures you're not overpaying for essential services.

On top of these primary tactics, here are some additional tips to maximize energy efficiency and mindful consumption (Stanger, 2024):

- **Insulate your home:** Proper insulation helps maintain indoor temperatures, reducing the need for heating and cooling. Insulating attics, walls, and floors can significantly impact energy savings.

- **Seal leaks:** Check windows and doors for drafts and seal leaks with weather-stripping or caulk. Preventing cold or hot air from entering your home keeps your HVAC system from working overtime.

- **Use energy-efficient appliances:** Whenever possible, replace old appliances with energy-efficient models. Look for the ENERGY STAR label, which indicates appliances that meet energy efficiency guidelines set by the EPA.

- **Install low-flow fixtures:** Reducing water consumption also cuts energy costs associated with heating water. Installing low-flow showerheads, faucets, and toilets can lead to substantial savings.

- **Plant shade trees:** Strategically planting trees around your home can provide natural cooling, reducing the strain on air conditioning systems during summer months.

Implementing these strategies requires initial effort and sometimes upfront costs but results in noticeable savings. It's important to involve all household members in these initiatives to ensure collective participation and success. Seeing reductions in monthly bills can motivate everyone to maintain these energy-efficient practices.

Finding Affordable Ways to Enjoy Leisure and Entertainment

One of the best ways to enjoy your free time without spending money is by exploring free community events. Many cities offer a variety of no-cost activities, such as concerts, fairs, farmers markets, and art exhibits. Local parks often host free movie nights or live music performances. These events provide entertainment and offer an excellent opportunity to connect with your community. Plus, checking the event calendars of nearby museums or cultural centers might reveal scheduled free admission days. Such experiences allow you to indulge in cultural enrichment without the financial burden.

Additionally, engaging in creative at-home activities is a fantastic way to have fun inexpensively. Hobbies such as painting, knitting, or gardening can be both enjoyable and therapeutic. You could pick up a good novel from the library (yes, borrowing books is still a thing!) and embark on an imaginary journey. Game nights are another great way to entertain yourself and your loved ones. Dust off those board games or try out new card games. DIY projects, whether it's crafting home décor or cooking exotic dishes, can also be very satisfying. These activities save money while teaching you new skills and providing a sense of accomplishment.

Also, potluck gatherings are a wonderful way to blend socializing with frugality. When you invite friends over for a potluck, everyone contributes a dish, which significantly reduces the individual cost of hosting. What's more, it adds variety to the meal and makes the gathering feel more collaborative. Prepare a cozy setting in your living room or backyard, light some candles, put on a playlist, and you've got yourself a simple yet delightful evening. This kind of gathering saves money and stimulates a sense of community and shared joy (Clampet, 2022).

Final Insights

In this chapter, we've discussed several savvy techniques that can help you save money on everyday expenses without compromising your quality of life. From harnessing the power of price comparison websites to signing up for retailer newsletters packed with exclusive deals, these techniques are all about getting more bang for your buck. We also discussed the magic of coupons and cashback apps, which make it feel like you're getting paid to shop. And let's not forget loyalty programs that reward you for frequent purchases, saving even more in the long run.

When you start incorporating these tactics into your daily routine, you'll watching the savings roll in. It's like finding extra cash in your pocket every time you shop. By making small adjustments—like using a comparison website before a big buy or checking those cluttered emails for hidden gems—you can turn these money-saving habits into second nature. So, with these practical tips, go forth and conquer your expenses, letting each little victory add up to significant savings over the long run. Saving money doesn't have to be a chore; with the right approach, it can be an exciting game of strategy and smart choices.

By adopting a frugal lifestyle rooted in minimalism, you can find joy not in what you accumulate but in what you let go. The upcoming chapter will explore how simplifying your life can unlock both financial freedom and deeper fulfillment.

UNIT 3: RESOURCES AND TOOLS

Digital marketplaces:
- Freelancer
- FlexJobs
- Toptal
- Behance
- Dribbble
- Upwork
- Fiverr
- Etsy

Price comparison websites:
- Google Shopping
- ShopMania
- Yahoo Shopping

Online courses and workshops:

- Teachable

- Thinkific

- Skillshare

E-book marketplaces:

- Amazon Kindle Direct Publishing

- Lulu

- IngramSpark

- Smashwords

UNIT 4: FRUGAL LIVING FOR A BETTER LIFE

CHAPTER 10

EMBRACING A FRUGAL MINDSET

Adopting a frugal mindset might seem about as exciting as reading the fine print on a contract, but it opens the door to greater happiness and freedom. A life without the constant pressure of financial worries allows for more purposeful spending, where each dollar goes toward something meaningful and every purchase truly enhances your well-being. Contrary to popular belief, this isn't about denying yourself life's pleasures or pinching pennies until they scream. Instead, it's about making smart choices that can lead to a richer, more fulfilling existence. Think of it as decluttering your finances—when you get rid of the unnecessary expenses, you make room for what truly matters.

How Frugality Can Lead to Greater Happiness and Freedom

Frugality often gets a bad rap, being seen as synonymous with deprivation and stinginess. But in reality, embracing a frugal mindset can lead to greater happiness and reduced stress. Making intentional choices about how we spend and save money lets us free ourselves from the constant worry of financial burdens and live a more fulfilling life.

First off, let's define frugality. It's not about denying yourself life's pleasures or living in perpetual austerity (Financial Samurai, 2024). Instead, it's a lifestyle choice focused on spending money wisely and prioritizing what truly matters. It allows you to cut through the noise and focus on what's important. Those who embrace this approach often find they gain clarity in their personal values, which in turn enhances their overall well-being.

A simplified life can lead to greater clarity in personal values. Can you imagine a clutter-free home where every item has a purpose and brings joy? This physical simplicity reflects an internal state of mind. When we strip away the excess, we make space for what truly matters—our health, relationships, personal growth, and passions. This mental clarity allows us to align our daily lives with our core values, leading to enhanced well-being.

For instance, by rejecting the societal pressure to constantly upgrade to the latest gadgets or fashion trends, we can focus on meaningful experiences and relationships. Rather than chasing material possessions, we can invest time and resources into activities that bring genuine joy and satisfaction. Studies have shown that people who value experiences over material goods report higher levels of happiness. The reason? Experiences create lasting memories and deepen connections with others, while material items often lose their appeal over time.

Adopting frugal habits can also lead to substantial savings. These savings can then be channeled toward investments or used to pay off debt, creating a sense of financial freedom. Instead of dining out frequently, preparing meals at home can save a significant amount of money over the course of a year. Those savings can then be put into a retirement fund, invested in stocks, or even used for a much-deserved vacation.

Take someone who decides to cut back on frequent shopping sprees. Consequently, these small changes accumulate into substantial savings. With fewer financial commitments, they might be able to pay off their student loans faster or build an emergency fund, reducing stress and providing peace of mind. Financial independence is within reach when one adopts a frugal lifestyle, paving the way for greater opportunities and less financial anxiety.

Another important aspect of frugality is the community and connection it cultivates among like-minded folks. Engaging with others who share similar values can be both motivating and educational. Joining a local frugality group or an online forum allows members to exchange tips, share their successes, and support each other when days are dark. These communities offer a treasure trove of knowledge and inspiration, making the journey towards financial independence less daunting and more enjoyable.

For instance, one might learn about DIY home repairs from a neighbor, saving hundreds of dollars on professional services. Or perhaps someone shares a tip on how to score great deals at thrift stores, allowing another to dress stylishly without breaking the bank. The shared learning experiences contribute to personal growth and reinforce the benefits of a frugal lifestyle.

These connections also break the isolation often associated with stringent budgeting. By sharing common goals and experiences, you create a support network that provides encouragement and accountability. Celebrating milestones, no matter how small, becomes a collective joy, reinforcing the positive aspects of a frugal lifestyle.

Pro Tips for Practicing Conscious Consumption

Recognizing wants versus needs is a fundamental step in making mindful purchasing decisions. Distinguishing between the two can help you prioritize your budget and ensure that your financial resources are allocated to what truly matters. While it's easy to justify buying the latest smartphone as a "need," taking a moment to consider whether your current phone still functions well can save you a significant amount of money (Practicing Mindful Consumerism, 2024).

Distinguishing Between Wants and Needs

Making this distinction becomes simpler with practice. Start by listing items you want to purchase and categorize them into "wants" and "needs." A need is something essential for your survival and well-being—think food, shelter, and healthcare. A want, on the other hand, is something that would be nice to have but isn't essential—like a new gadget or trendy clothes. By regularly evaluating your purchases through this lens, you'll become more adept at avoiding unnecessary expenditures.

Comparing Prices and Quality

Once you've identified your needs and wants, take time to compare prices and quality before making any purchase. This practice helps you make better financial decisions, while demonstrating responsibility in managing your money. Think of it as being a savvy shopper; just because something is on sale doesn't mean it's a good deal. Spend a few minutes researching online reviews or comparing products in different stores. You'll often find that spending a little extra time can result in significant savings or a higher-quality product that lasts longer. Here are some price comparison websites you could use:

- PriceGrabber

- Google Shopping

- Shopzilla

- Kelkoo

- Idealo

Supporting Ethical Brands and Local Businesses

When you choose to buy from companies that prioritize fair labor practices, environmental sustainability, and corporate responsibility, you're sending a message about your values. Plus, supporting local businesses helps foster a sense of community and promotes economic stability in your area. It's like hitting two birds with one stone—you get what you need while contributing to a larger cause. To identify ethical brands, do a bit of research on the companies you frequently buy from. Look for certifications such as Fair Trade, B Corp, or organic labels that indicate a commitment to sustainable and ethical practices. Local businesses often advertise their goods as locally sourced, so you can feel good knowing your money stays within your community. These choices might sometimes come at a premium, but knowing you're contributing to a more sustainable future can make the extra cost worthwhile.

Creating Spending Limits

Setting a budget for discretionary spending ensures you don't overspend and helps you live within your means. Consider using the aforementioned apps or simple spreadsheets to track your spending. Allocate specific amounts for various categories such as groceries, entertainment, and dining out. This way, you'll have a clear picture of where your money is going and can make adjustments as needed. Just because you put a cap on your spending doesn't mean you're signing up for a life that's all beans and no burritos. Instead, it's about making conscious choices that reflect your priorities. If your love for weekend getaways is draining your savings, consider swapping those costly trips for local adventures or exploring nearby parks and attractions. Setting aside some money for occasional splurges can help you stick to your budget without feeling completely restricted.

Bringing It All Together

Incorporating these practices might seem like trying to teach a cat to fetch, but think of it as laying the groundwork for a future where your well-being gets an upgrade and stress takes a permanent vacation. Mindful consumerism doesn't require making perfect choices every time; it emphasizes making better, more informed choices over time. Reflect on how each purchase aligns with your long-term goals and values. If you make mistakes along the way, view them as learning experiences rather than failures.

Let's talk about the emotional benefits of these changes as well. When you know your spending aligns with your values, it brings peace and satisfaction. You'll find that making thought-out decisions reduces buyer's remorse and increases overall life satisfaction. Also, knowing you're contributing to ethical causes and local economies can add an extra layer of fulfillment.

Reflecting on your shopping experience can offer valuable insights too. After each purchase, take a moment to think about how it made you feel and whether it aligned with your values. Did buying that high-quality, ethically made item make you happier than a cheaper alternative would have? Use these reflections to guide future decisions, gradually building a habit of mindful shopping.

Understanding needs versus wants, comparing prices and quality, supporting ethical brands, and setting spending limits are all practical steps towards adopting a frugal mindset. Each of these strategies supports both financial health and personal satisfaction, creating a balanced approach to consumerism. As you implement these tips, you'll discover that mindful purchasing doesn't just benefit your wallet—it enriches your life.

The Financial and Emotional Benefits of Minimalism

Embracing a frugal mindset through minimalism can significantly transform various aspects of your life, offering both emotional and financial rewards. Focusing on quality over quantity is like trading in a cluttered toolbox for a few well-chosen, high-quality tools. It clears the way for a more streamlined life, where both your space and your mind can breathe easier.

Minimalism encourages us to prioritize quality over quantity in every facet of life. Rather than accumulating numerous items that offer fleeting satisfaction, a minimalist approach emphasizes investing in fewer, higher-quality possessions that provide long-term value and joy. This shift in mindset allows for more thoughtful decision-making and leads to an enriched life experience. Opting for one sturdy piece of furniture instead of a bunch of flimsy ones is like choosing to buy a reliable car instead of a dozen rental scooters. It makes your space look sharp and keeps you from constantly replacing the latest "deal of the week," saving you both cash and headaches.

Financially, minimalism naturally leads to lower expenses, which translates to reduced financial stress. When we embrace a minimalist lifestyle, our spending habits change markedly. We become more intentional about our purchases, steering clear of impulsive buys that add little value to our lives. As Rachel Jones notes, this paradigm shift helps us view possessions as tools rather than goals, minimizing the urge to splurge on items that might only end up collecting dust (Jones, n.d.). Consequently, our financial resources are better allocated toward essential needs, savings, or investments that can secure our future.

Living minimally promotes mental clarity and diminishes feelings of overwhelm. Cluttered spaces often contribute to increased stress and anxiety, making it difficult to focus and function effectively. Eliminating excess belongings creates a serene and orderly space that induces mental peace. Findings published in *Personality and Social Psychology Bulletin* claimed that "women who described their homes as less cluttered and more organized experienced a decrease in depressed mood over the course of the day" (Travers, 2023). This indicates that a minimalist home setting can significantly uplift one's emotional state, providing a stable foundation for productivity and personal growth.

Minimalism also places a strong emphasis on valuing experiences over possessions, establishing deeper connections, and creating fulfilling memories. In a consumer-driven society, it's easy to get caught up in the cycle of acquiring material goods in the hope of achieving happiness. However, experiences such as travel, learning new skills, or spending quality time with loved ones bring more lasting joy than tangible items. Experiences forge meaningful bonds with others, enriching our lives with treasured memories that far outlast the fleeting pleasure derived from material acquisitions.

Final Insights

By now, we've deeply delved into the realm of frugality and discovered its hidden treasures. Embracing a frugal lifestyle isn't about tightening your purse strings or living below the breadline; it's about focusing on what truly matters and finding joy in simplicity. From rejecting unnecessary upgrades to making intentional choices that align with our values, we've learned that frugality can lead to greater happiness and financial freedom. Clearing away the clutter—both physical and mental—opens up space for what genuinely enriches our lives, whether it's meaningful experiences or nurturing important relationships.

As you journey down this avenue, remember that adopting frugality doesn't mean going it alone. The support of like-minded folks can make all the difference, transforming hitches and snags into shared learning experiences and victories into collective celebrations. With fewer financial stressors and a focus on quality over quantity, you'll find that both your wallet and well-being benefit. Embracing minimalism and mindful consumption leads to a life that's not just financially smart but also deeply satisfying. So, here's to living simply, spending wisely, and cherishing what truly counts!

In the next chapter, you'll learn how taking on DIY projects and embracing upcycling can be both a wallet-friendly and eco-friendly choice. Discover how these creative endeavors can save you money and turn you into a household wizard with a knack for sustainability. You'll impress your friends with your DIY skills and make Mother Earth proud, all while saving a few bucks.

CHAPTER 11

DIY AND UPCYCLING

Engaging in DIY projects and upcycling can turn your otherwise mundane weekends into exciting adventures of creativity and sustainability. You can transform that old, forgotten piece of furniture into a stylish home upgrade—saving money, reducing waste, and making your friends wonder if you've got a secret design degree. The allure of crafting something unique with your own hands is irresistible, especially when the finished product reflects your personal style and ingenuity. Plus, there's nothing quite like the satisfaction of stepping back and admiring something you've made yourself, knowing that it didn't come with a hefty price tag or contribute to environmental degradation.

How DIY Projects Can Save Money and Boost Creativity

Do-it-yourself endeavors offer both practical and creative benefits, making them an attractive option for anyone looking to save money and express their individuality. Jumping into DIY can save you some cash and let you unleash your inner artist, proving that you're not just handy with a hammer but also a maestro of creativity.

Cost-Effectiveness

Many premade items, whether they're home décor or essential repairs, are a pricey expense due to labor and manufacturing costs. When you take on these projects yourself, you can eliminate those expenses, often saving hundreds of dollars. Building a custom bookshelf or revamping old furniture costs significantly less than buying new pieces at retail prices. With a bit of research and effort, you can source affordable materials that fit your budget without compromising quality (Community Challenges or Contests, 2024).

Positive Impacts on Your Mental Health

The process of creating something with your hands can be incredibly therapeutic. Engaging in crafting activities like knitting, painting, or woodworking allows you to focus solely on the task at hand, promoting mindfulness and relaxation. Completing a DIY project can boost your self-esteem and provide a welcome break from everyday stress, proving you're not just a master at managing work deadlines and grocery lists but also at transforming old stuff into something fantastic. The act of being creative can reduce stress levels and encourage a more positive outlook on life (Mendoza, 2023).

Innovation and Resourcefulness

Thrift stores, garage sales, and even your own household items can become treasure troves of potential DIY supplies. An old ladder can be repurposed into a one-of-a-kind bookshelf, and mason jars can be turned into stylish candle holders—proving that one person's trash is another's chance to impress their friends. This approach saves money and reduces waste by repurposing items that might otherwise end up in the landfill. It's inspiring to see how everyday objects can be given a new lease on life through a bit of creativity and elbow grease.

DIY Workshops and Community Projects

Participating in DIY workshops and community projects offer opportunities to learn new techniques and share ideas with others who have similar interests. Whether it's joining a local crafting circle or attending a woodworking class, these experiences can introduce you to different perspectives and innovative approaches. Collaborating with others on projects can lead to lasting friendships and a sense of community. Working on a communal garden or joining a neighborhood repair day fosters a team spirit that's good for everyone involved—because nothing says "community bonding" like fixing fences and planting flowers together (Community Challenges or Contests, 2024).

Educational Value

Each project helps develop a new set of skills, from basic carpentry to intricate sewing techniques. As you gain experience, you'll find yourself better equipped to tackle increasingly complex tasks with confidence and competence. This incremental learning process enhances your self-sufficiency; knowing that you can fix or create things on your own empowers you to handle future challenges more effectively. The problem-solving skills you develop are invaluable—after all, if you can fix a squeaky door, you're definitely ready to handle the complex task of figuring out why your Wi-Fi decides to disappear every time you need it (Mendoza, 2023).

Complete Customization

DIY projects allow you to tailor items precisely to your taste. Unlike mass-produced goods, which often lack that personalized *je ne sais quoi*, DIY creations reflect your unique style and preferences. This customization makes your living space truly feel like home and showcases your personality through one-of-a-kind pieces.

Sustainable Practices

Opting to create and repurpose items allows you to contribute to reducing waste and minimizing your carbon footprint. Instead of buying new products that require resources and energy to manufacture, you make use of what already exists.

This mindset not only supports sustainability but also encourages a culture of frugality and responsible consumption. It's a win-win situation: You save money while making environmentally conscious choices (Community Challenges or Contests, 2024).

Family Bonding

Involving your loved ones in hands-on activities like building a birdhouse or planting a garden provides quality time together. These shared experiences create lasting memories and teach valuable lessons about teamwork, patience, and perseverance. Children, in particular, can benefit from participating in DIY projects. They learn practical skills and gain a deeper understanding of the effort required to bring ideas to life. This hands-on learning complements traditional education, turning abstract concepts into something you can literally get your hands on—because nothing says "I understand physics" like building a working model rocket from scratch.

Sharing Your DIY Journey

Many enthusiasts document their projects on blogs, social media, or YouTube, inspiring others to embark on their own DIY adventures. This exchange of ideas fosters a global community of creators who support and motivate each other. Seeing the diverse range of projects and solutions people come up with can ignite your creativity and push you to explore new avenues. Here are some DIY blog websites:

- The Spruce Crafts

- Craftsy

- DIY Network

- HomeTalk

Monetizing DIY Hobbies

For those looking to turn their DIY hobbies into a business, workshops can provide the foundational skills needed for entrepreneurship. Learning how to make soap, candles, jewelry, or furniture can spark ideas for a small business venture. The initial investment in tools and materials can be offset by the potential revenue from selling handmade items. They say if you love what you do, you'll never work a day in your life, and there's nothing like getting paid for something you'd do for free, if only you could afford to (Mendoza, 2023).

DIY projects highlight the importance of patience and dedication. Unlike instant gratification from purchasing ready-made items, crafting something yourself requires time and effort. This process teaches valuable life lessons about perseverance and the joy of achieving long-term goals. Each completed masterpiece showcases your hard work and determination, reinforcing the belief that you can accomplish anything you set your mind to.

Pro Tips for Turning Old Items Into New Treasures

Upcycling, a creative and innovative approach to sustainability, provides significant financial savings while benefiting the planet. Simple techniques can transform old furniture or household items into stylish décor, breathing new life into otherwise discarded pieces. For example, take an old wooden chair and sand it down, slap on some fresh paint, and reupholster it to match modern trends.

It's like giving your furniture a makeover show, reducing waste and proving that even chairs deserve a second chance at fabulousness.

Concrete examples highlighting the cost differential between new items and upcycled versions emphasize the financial benefits of upcycling. Purchasing a new dresser can cost several hundred dollars, whereas finding an old one at a thrift store and applying a fresh coat of paint can cost significantly less. What's more, upcycling plays a crucial role in reducing landfill waste, offering a sustainable solution to environmental concerns. Giving items a second life keeps them out of landfills, conserves resources, and reduces pollution. It's like giving Mother Nature a break because every piece you repurpose is one less thing she has to clean up. Upcycling aligns with the principles of a circular economy, where materials are reused and repurposed, reducing the demand for new raw materials (The Benefits of Upcycling, n.d.).

Participation in DIY workshops and community projects can further enrich the upcycling experience. Joining local classes or online groups offers opportunities to gain new skills and share tips with like-minded folks. Collaborating with friends or neighbors on larger projects can significantly reduce costs. Building lasting friendships around shared interests in frugality and creativity adds another layer of satisfaction; when you team up with a partner in crime who's as thrilled about finding bargains and crafting as you are, every budget-friendly victory feels like a shared triumph.

Connecting With Others Who Share Frugal Values

Engaging in DIY projects and upcycling is more than just a fun pastime; it's a gateway to saving money, promoting sustainability, and stimulating creativity. One of the most rewarding aspects of this experience is the relationships built along the way. Forming connections with like-minded people can greatly enhance motivation, inspire fresh ideas, and create a support network that makes the experience even more enriching (Majumdar, 2018).

Joining groups that focus on frugality and DIY projects is an excellent starting point. These communities are like a secret arsenal of resources and knowledge, supercharging your efforts and making your journey through frugality and creativity a whole lot smoother and more informed. Sharing experiences, tips, and materials makes projects more economical and introduces you to new techniques and perspectives you might not have considered on your own. In many cases, these groups operate both online and offline, offering flexibility for everyone to participate. From Facebook groups to local meet-ups, there's a wealth of opportunities to connect with others who share your passion for DIY and upcycling.

In these communities, the collective wisdom and enthusiasm create a milieu where new ideas flourish. You might discover innovative ways to repurpose items or get advice on tackling a troublesome project. Community experiences can be incredibly inspiring, sparking new ideas and pushing you to try things outside your comfort zone. Witnessing someone turn an old dresser into a chic piece of furniture can be like seeing a magic trick—it inspires you to tackle your own projects with the same enthusiasm and creativity. The support and encouragement from group members can be invaluable, especially when you hit a creative block or feel overwhelmed by a project.

Offering classes and creating collaborative projects within these communities further enhances the learning experience. Classes can range from beginner workshops on basic DIY skills to advanced sessions on specific techniques like furniture restoration or eco-friendly crafting. These educational opportunities not only help you pick up new skills but also give your confidence a much-needed boost. Meanwhile, collaborative projects bring people together with a common goal, turning group work into a chance to share triumphs—and the occasional battle over who forgot to bring the glue. Imagine a group project transforming a communal space like a park or community center using upcycled materials; such initiatives not only beautify the area but also exemplify the power of collective effort.

Another significant benefit of these communities is their potential for environmental and community-based improvements. When folks come together with a shared interest in sustainability, the impact can be profound. Collective efforts in DIY and upcycling contribute to reducing waste, conserving resources, and promoting responsible consumption. Organizing swap events for materials allows participants to exchange items they no longer need, reducing the demand for new resources and minimizing waste. Community challenges that encourage creative repurposing of everyday items can also promote innovation and sustainable practices on a broader scale.

The mutual growth experienced in these communities extends beyond just acquiring new skills. It encompasses a deeper understanding of frugality and responsible consumption, making these ideals more accessible and actionable. Engaging in discussions about sustainability, sharing success stories, and celebrating small victories together helps reinforce these values and keep everyone motivated. This shared responsibility gives you a sense of purpose and fulfillment, knowing that your individual efforts contribute to a bigger picture—a collective quest for a more sustainable future. Think of it as being part of a team where everyone's doing their part, and no one has to worry about the copier jamming.

Creating a culture of mentorship within these groups is another powerful way to build relationships and ensure the continuity of skills and knowledge. Experienced members can guide newcomers, helping them tackle their first projects and avoid common pitfalls. This support system creates a welcoming atmosphere where everyone feels included and valued, making you feel like part of a friendly gang where even the shyest member gets a high-five and a slice of pizza. Mentorship also encourages continuous learning and improvement, as seasoned DIYers pass down their expertise and best practices to the next generation of aficionados.

For those looking to enhance their DIY journey, finding and participating in these communities can make all the difference. These groups don't just offer practical perks like resource sharing and skill development; they also provide emotional and social support, making them as essential as a trusty toolkit and a good chat over coffee.

Final Insights

Alright, we've covered the practical and creative benefits of DIY and upcycling in this chapter. From saving a large wad of cash to giving your mental well-being a boost, these projects are like the Swiss Army knife of hobbies. We've also seen how resourceful you can get with materials—who knew an old wine crate could be transformed into a chic side table? And don't forget, these projects can be a ticket to some top-notch family bonding time, all while reducing waste and flexing those innovative muscles.

Now, as you ponder your next weekend project, remember that you're not just crafting or fixing things—you're part of a larger movement toward sustainability and financial savviness. Whether you're joining a local workshop or swapping ideas online with fellow DIY enthusiasts, you're building a community that's as supportive as it is creative. So, go ahead—unleash your inner artist, save some bucks, and maybe even make a few new friends along the way. Your odyssey into the world of DIY and upcycling awaits!

Now that you've wrapped your head around DIY projects, it's time to shift focus to the bigger picture of long-term savings. Next, you'll discover how integrating sustainability into your daily life benefits the planet while helping you save money over the long haul.

CHAPTER 12
SUSTAINABLE CHOICES FOR LONG-TERM SAVINGS

Living a green life while securing financial freedom isn't just possible—it's an adventure worth jumping into. You swap out your old habits for eco-friendly choices, and suddenly your wallet starts feeling like it's been on a growth spurt, all while you're doing your bit for the planet. By embracing small changes like energy-efficient appliances and second-hand shopping, you can save money and help the environment at the same time. You'll find that tweaking your daily routine doesn't just benefit your bank account; it's also a step towards a more sustainable future.

Pro Tips for Saving Money While Being Environmentally Conscious

Integrating sustainable living into your personal finance is a win-win that can save you money while keeping your eco-friendly values intact. By making thoughtful decisions about energy use, transportation, shopping habits, and home gardening, you can carve out a path to financial freedom that's as rewarding as finding extra cash in your old jeans (Environmental Center, 2024).

Embracing Energy Efficiency

One of the simplest yet most impactful ways to save money and reduce your carbon footprint is by embracing energy efficiency. Switching to energy-efficient appliances is a great starting point. For instance, replacing an old refrigerator with an ENERGY STAR-certified model can save you up to $300 over five years on utility bills. Similarly, LED lightbulbs consume significantly less energy than traditional incandescent bulbs and last much longer, reducing replacement costs over time. Small lifestyle adjustments also contribute to energy conservation. Using a clothesline instead of a dryer or washing clothes in cold water can lower electricity usage. These changes may seem minor, but collectively, they add up to notable savings on your monthly utility bill.

Utilizing Public Transportation

The rising costs associated with owning a car—insurance premiums, fuel expenses, maintenance, and parking fees—can quickly drain your budget. Exploring public transportation options saves money while promoting sustainability. Buses, subways, and trains provide cost-effective alternatives that reduce the need for personal vehicle use.

In many urban areas, public transit systems are well-developed and offer efficient routes to key destinations. Monthly or annual transit passes are typically more affordable than the cumulative costs of driving. Comparing the average cost of a monthly transit pass to expenses like gas, oil changes, and insurance reveals significant potential savings. Plus, eliminating the stress of daily driving and contributing to reduced traffic congestion can enhance overall quality of life.

Bike-sharing programs and ride-sharing services offer additional flexible transportation options. Many cities have invested in bike lanes and shared paths, making cycling a safe and economical way to traverse the urban landscape.

Ride-sharing services can be particularly beneficial for those occasional trips when public transport isn't convenient, allowing you to forego the expense of car ownership while still having access to a vehicle when necessary.

Buying Secondhand

Whether you're looking for clothing, furniture, electronics, or other household items, buying pre-owned can drastically cut costs. Thrift stores, consignment shops, garage sales, and online marketplaces like Gumtree, eBay, Facebook Marketplace and Craigslist offer an abundance of gently used goods at a fraction of their original price.

Purchasing second-hand helps extend the lifespan of products, reducing the demand for new manufacturing. This practice cuts down on resource extraction, production emissions, and waste generation. For example, buying a high-quality used sofa instead of a brand-new one saves you money and keeps you from shelling out for something that might have looked perfect in the showroom but turns out to be a three-month wonder.

Many communities host swap meets or clothing exchanges, where you can trade items you no longer need for something you do. This cultivates a sense of community and introduces you to frugal living enthusiasts who can share tips and insights.

Online platforms also offer opportunities to buy and sell secondhand items locally. Facebook Marketplace and apps like OfferUp make it easy to find pre-loved treasures right in your neighborhood. These platforms come with user reviews and ratings, so you can shop with confidence—after all, nothing says "peace of mind" like reading through a million reviews to ensure you're not accidentally buying a vintage toaster that's also a time machine.

Home and Garden Sustainability

Transforming your living space into a hub of sustainability offers numerous rewards, including financial savings, better health, and a deeper connection to nature. Home gardening is a prime example of how integrating green practices can yield tangible benefits.

- Growing your own fruits, vegetables, and herbs reduces grocery bills and ensures a steady supply of fresh produce. Even with limited space, container gardens or vertical gardening systems can be quite productive. Learning basic gardening skills is relatively easy, and numerous resources are available online or through local community workshops.

- Composting is another practice that complements home gardening. By recycling kitchen scraps and yard waste into nutrient-rich compost, you can improve soil health and reduce the need for chemical fertilizers. This lowers gardening costs and diverts organic waste from landfills, reducing methane emissions.

- Rainwater harvesting is another method that conserves resources and cuts expenses. Setting up a rain barrel system to collect runoff from your roof provides a free source of water for your garden.

- Xeriscaping—a landscaping technique that uses drought-tolerant plants—further enhances water efficiency, reducing both water bills and maintenance efforts. Implementing these practices creates a resilient and cost-effective outdoor space.

- Indoor sustainability initiatives are equally impactful. For example, indoor plants improve air quality and create a calming atmosphere, which can enhance mental well-being and productivity.

- Opting for natural cleaning products, many of which can be made from simple ingredients like vinegar and baking soda, can also lower household expenses and minimize exposure to harmful chemicals.

Pro Tips for Planning for Future Financial Needs with a Frugal Approach

Adopting a frugal mindset can be like giving your financial planning a turbo boost. By embracing minimalistic values, you save money and make intentional choices, turning your budget from a tightrope walk into a well-paved path toward long-term sustainability (Why Frugality, 2024).

Creating Emergency Fund Savings

One of the first steps toward financial security is establishing an emergency fund. This might seem daunting at first, but think of small, consistent savings as the financial equivalent of saving your loose change in a jar. Over time, those little coins can add up to a hefty stash—kind of like turning your spare pennies into a mini fortune, one clink at a time. Start by setting aside a fixed amount from your paycheck each month. An emergency fund acts like a financial buffer, covering unexpected expenses such as medical emergencies, car repairs, or job loss. This approach is not just about stashing away money; it helps you build peace of mind. You don't need to start with large sums. Even saving $10 a week can grow considerably over a year, and eventually, you'll find it easier to increase this amount.

Investing in Reliability

While spending more upfront on durable items might seem counterintuitive to saving, it's actually a smart move. High-quality products tend to last longer, reducing the need for frequent replacements. Buying a pair of shoes that cost double what you'd usually spend but lasts four times as long is like paying for a high-end gym membership that guarantees you'll actually use it. Investing more upfront saves you from constantly replacing things. Not only do you save money in the long run, but you also reduce waste, contributing to environmental sustainability.

Long-Term Sustainable Investing

When it comes to growing your wealth, consider sustainable investing. Putting your money into eco-friendly companies promises potential returns and aligns with ethical values. Sustainable investing means supporting businesses that prioritize environmental responsibility, social contributions, and good governance. It's a way to ensure your investments reflect your personal values while working toward financial growth. Companies with strong sustainability practices tend to perform better financially over the long term. The market demand for environmentally conscious products is growing, and being part of this movement can offer substantial returns. Look into mutual funds or ETFs that focus on sustainable industries, such as renewable energy or green technology. These investments aren't just forward-thinking—they're like choosing a reusable coffee cup over a mountain of disposable ones, benefiting both your wallet and a cleaner, healthier planet.

Retirement Planning with a Frugal Mindset

Planning for retirement might seem far off, but it's crucial to start early, especially with a frugal mindset. Contributing consistently to a retirement savings plan can significantly boost your future financial security. Taking full advantage of employer matches is essentially free money that can grow your nest egg substantially (Payne, 2022). Living frugally now can significantly boost the longevity of your retirement funds. It's like stretching a meal to feed a crowd—by practicing mindful spending and saving, you can make your retirement income last longer without feeling like you're dining on plain rice and beans every day.

Final Insights

This chapter has taken you on a rollercoaster ride of eco-friendly financial wisdom, showing that saving the planet and your money can go hand in hand. From upgrading to energy-efficient appliances and embracing public transportation to making second-hand purchases and transforming your home into a green haven, you've learned how small, mindful choices add up to big savings. By integrating green living into your daily routine, you're setting yourself up for a future where financial freedom and environmental responsibility coexist harmoniously.

As you implement these strategies, remember that every little effort counts. Whether it's hanging your laundry to dry, biking instead of driving, or growing your own veggies, these actions are powerful steps toward a more sustainable and frugal lifestyle. The journey might require some adjustments and occasional sacrifices, but the rewards are worth it—both for your wallet and the world. So, go ahead, make those green decisions, and watch as they lead you down the path to both financial security and a healthier planet.

UNIT 4: RESOURCES AND TOOLS

Online marketplaces:

- Gumtree

- eBay

- Facebook Marketplace

- Craigslist

- OfferUp

Price comparison websites:

- PriceGrabber

- Google Shopping

- Shopzilla

- Kelkoo

- Idealo

DIY blog websites

- The Spruce Crafts

- Craftsy

- DIY Network

- HomeTalk

- Poppy & Bliss

CONCLUSION

As you reach the end of this delightful romp through the land of personal finance, take a moment to pat yourself on the back. Seriously, do it now—you deserve it. Can you recall that time when tracking your spending was only slightly less confusing than deciphering a toddler's drawing of the family dog? Well, look at you now, conquering spreadsheets and budgeting apps like a pro. Reflect on those early victories—no matter how tiny they seemed—and use them as a motivational booster shot for the road ahead.

Let's face it, mastering your money is like navigating through a dense jungle. There will be unexpected bumps, like splurging on a "necessary" gadget or having to repair your leaky faucet (who knew water could be so insidious?). But every hurdle is a stepping stone toward greater financial wisdom. When you faced the horrors of impulse buying and triumphed with nothing but sheer willpower and maybe some hideous but free promotional pens, you laid down bricks for your path to financial independence.

So, what comes next? Setting goals, my financially savvy friend! Envision your dream vacation—perhaps sipping piña coladas on a beach where your biggest worry is how many times the sunblock needs reapplying. This isn't just fantasy; it can be your reality. By setting specific, measurable goals, you turn daydreams into actionable aspirations. Being intentional about your financial objectives means deciding what matters most to you and allocating your resources accordingly.

Start by identifying exactly how much that dream vacation will cost. Divide the sum into manageable monthly savings targets. Suddenly, it doesn't look so horrifying anymore. By consistently putting aside that little bit each month, gradually, you'll get there without breaking a sweat—or, more importantly, your bank account.

Of course, life's unpredictability will occasionally throw curveballs your way. Don't sweat it. The trick is flexibility. When unforeseen expenses pop up, revisit your priorities and adjust. The key is to remain focused on your long-term vision while being adaptable in your approach.

Never stop learning. Financial literacy isn't a one-time achievement to be set aside like a forgotten relic. It's an evolving skill that requires consistent attention, much like tending to a well-maintained garden. No, dear friend, think of it as a never-ending story, where each chapter brings new lessons and exciting twists. Today, you're learning about budgeting, tomorrow might be investments, and who knows, next year you could be exploring the mysteries of cryptocurrency or sustainable investing.

To stay informed, continuously seek out new resources. Listen to podcasts, read books, follow financial blogs—all in the name of keeping your knowledge fresh. Be curious, and don't settle for the bare minimum. The financial landscape is ever-changing, and staying up-to-date empowers you to make informed decisions that benefit your wallet in the long run.

Creating a supportive community around your financial journey can also make a world of difference. Going solo might seem appealing if you've got a healthy distrust of humanity's ability to give good advice, but trust me, sharing the burden lightens the load. Whether it's joining online forums, local community groups, or just having regular financial check-ins with friends, these connections provide motivation, accountability, and shared experiences.

You could very well be chatting with a buddy about your latest budgeting triumph or comparing notes on minimalist living. Not only does this create a sense of camaraderie, but it also opens doors to new strategies and perspectives. You'll soon find that others' successes and failures are powerful learning tools. Plus, celebrating financial milestones together makes the journey feel less like a slog through a swamp and more like a hike with scenic overlooks.

And let's not forget the therapeutic value of venting to someone who truly understands the pain of an unexpected car repair bill. A strong support system cushions the blows and provides reassurance that you're not alone in this quest for financial stability. Together, you and your allies can explore new horizons, surmount hurdles, and emerge victorious.

In closing, embrace your financial journey with enthusiasm and optimism. Laugh at your past mistakes as treasured war stories. Reward yourself for milestones, no matter how small. Start saving for those big dreams and keep expanding your financial education. Surround yourself with a community that lifts you up and keeps you accountable.

Managing your money isn't about depriving yourself or slogging through endless sacrifices. It's about making conscious choices that align with your values and priorities. It's about finding freedom and joy in knowing where your money goes and having the power to direct it toward what truly matters to you. With every step you take, you're not just improving your financial situation; you're crafting a life that you can savor, one wise decision at a time.

So, go forth with confidence, armed with a hearty dose of knowledge. Your financial adventure awaits, filled with both ups and downs. Just remember to enjoy the ride because, after all, it's not just about the destination—it's also about the ridiculous, enlightening, and enriching journey along the way. Here's to your financial success and all the laughter that accompanies it!

YOU'RE AWESOME FOR MAKING IT TO THE END!

Thank you for letting us join you on your financial journey! If this book brightened your day and helped you on the path to smarter spending, consider leaving a **review on Amazon**. Every review helps reach more people who might need a little financial inspiration. Here's to smart spending, happy living, and more books to come!

REFERENCES

Ahmed, A. (2021, April 21). *The culture of money*. Oban International. https://obaninternational.com/blog/the-culture-of-money/

An essential guide to building an emergency fund. (n.d.). Consumer Financial Protection Bureau. https://www.consumerfinance.gov/an-essential-guide-to-building-an-emergency-fund/

Anderson, S. (n.d.). *Building an emergency fund: Your financial safety net*. CPAs and Business Advisors. https://www.cbmcpa.com/2024/07/18/building-emergency-fund-financial-safety-net/

Batch, K. (2024, May 10). *Annual financial review: Why you need a personal financial review*. Financial Insights for Individuals and Businesses. https://blog.umb.com/annual-financial-reviews-financial-review-edu-con/

Blaine, T. (2024, July 10). *Needs vs. wants: How to budget for both*. Stash Learn. https://www.stash.com/learn/needs-vs-wants/

Career development and employee satisfaction. (2024, August 12). Accurate Australia. https://www.accurate.com/au/blog/career-development/

Clampet, J. (2022, January 30). *200+ event ideas to steal today*. Skift Meetings; Skift Meetings. https://meetings.skift.com/2022/01/30/event-ideas/

Coinfella. (2023, September 22). *10 tips on managing irregular income with ease as a freelancer*. Medium; Medium. https://medium.com/@coinfella/10-tips-on-managing-irregular-income-with-ease-as-a-freelancer-e6d78b47618a

Community challenges or contests: DIY workshops: Handmade happiness: The bonding of DIY workshops. (2024, June 14). https://fastercapital.com/content/Community-challenges-or-contests--DIY -Workshops--Handmade-Happiness--The-Bonding-of-DIY-Workshops.html

Cross, A. (2024, August 19). *Bonusly | the benefits and perks your company should be offering.* Bonusly.com. https://bonusly.com/post/benefits-and-perks

Environmental Center. (2024, March 27). *How to save money with sustainable choices.* Division of Student Affairs. https://www.colorado.edu/studentaffairs/2024/03/27/how-save-money-su stainable-choices

Experiences make people happier than material goods, says University of Colorado prof. (2004, December 28). ScienceDaily. https://www.sciencedaily.com/releases/2004/12/041219182811.htm

Facet. (2024, January 9). *5 smart ways to use or spend your bonus.* Facet. https://facet.com/career/5-smart-ways-to-use-or-spend-your-bonus/

FAIRWINDS. (2023). *Why celebrating your financial wins is important.* FAIRWINDS Credit Union; FAIRWINDS Credit Union. https://www.fairwinds.org/articles/why-celebrating-your-financial-wins-is-i mportant

Fargo, S. (2024, March 15). *6 mindful breathing exercises.* Mindfulness Exercises. https://mindfulnessexercises.com/6-mindful-breathing-exercises/

Financial Samurai. (2024, June 22). *Stop frugality from leading to lifestyle deflation.* Financial Samurai. https://www.financialsamurai.com/stop-frugality-from-leading-to-lifestyle-deflation/

5 simple automated business ideas for passive income in 2024. (2024). Getmagical.com. https://www.getmagical.com/blog/automated-business--ideas-for-passive-i ncome

Frugal living: The art of frugality: Living well on less according to financial planning authors. (2024, June 24). FasterCapital.

https://www.fastercapital.com/content/Frugal-Living--The-Art-of-Frugality-Living-Well-on-Less-According-to-Financial-Planning-Authors.html

Grieve, C. (n.d.). *How to use the digital envelope system in 6 steps.* North One Blog. https://www.northone.com/blog/accounting/digital-envelope-system

Grobler, E. (2024, September 4). *8 expert-approved techniques to cut your gas, electric and water costs.* CNET. https://www.cnet.com/home/energy-and-utilities/8-expert-approved-techniques-to-cut-your-gas-electric-and-water-costs/

Holzhauer, B. (2021, May 26). *The best budgeting apps of june 2021.* Forbes Advisor. https://www.forbes.com/advisor/banking/best-budgeting-apps/

Jones, R. (n.d.). *How minimalism frees up emotions, finances & time {the benefits of minimalism part 2}.* Nourishing Minimalism. https://nourishingminimalism.com/minimalism-emotions-finances-time/

Luthi, B. (2023, November 22). *5 types of budget plans to know about.* Experian. https://www.experian.com/blogs/ask-experian/types-of-budget-plans/

Majumdar, P. (2018). *Motivation for do-it-yourself in rural base of the pyramid communities and the changing landscape.* ResearchGate. https://www.researchgate.net/publication/327968152_Motivation_for_Do-It-Yourself_in_Rural_Base_of_the_Pyramid_Communities_and_the_Changing_Landscape

Mapfre, R. (2023, December 18). *Emotional spending: what is it and how to manage it?* MAPFRE. https://www.mapfre.com/en/insights/economy/emotional-spending/

Marter, J. (2023, May 12). *The psychology of emotional spending | psychology today.* Www.psychologytoday.com. https://www.psychologytoday.com/us/blog/mental-wealth/202305/the-psychology-of-emotional-spending

McMullen, L. (2024, August 12). *The 7 best budget apps for 2021.* NerdWallet. https://www.nerdwallet.com/article/finance/best-budget-apps

Mendoza, V. (2023, May 20). *DIY day: A celebration of creativity and resourcefulness.* Cottage Corner; Cottage corner. https://www.cottage-corner.com/post/diy-day-a-celebration-of-creativity-and-resourcefulness?srsltid=AfmBOorWqJGKGjEBUdAKFRMmWLQTcuNEHwfSCKEjUZCAtosa8Lgytlxh

Niedt, B. (2021, March 1). *17 deal sites and tools for finding online shopping bargains.* Kiplinger.com; Kiplinger. https://www.kiplinger.com/personal-finance/shopping/online-shopping/601523/deal-sites-and-tools-for-finding-online-bargains

Ossevoort, N. (2024, April 4). *Choosing the best employee benefits package: 5 essential components.* BPAS. https://www.bpas.com/blog/employee-benefits/

Payne, K. (2022, September 27). *Best places to keep your emergency fund.* Forbes Advisor. https://www.forbes.com/advisor/banking/best-places-to-keep-your-emergency-fund/

Practicing mindful consumerism for a balanced life. (2024, July 29). Zenify. https://zenify.exblog.jp/242593691/

Quicken Simplifi: Personal finance made powerfully simple. (n.d.). Quicken. https://www.quicken.com/products/simplifi/

Ross, N. (2013, November 19). *The effects of family culture on family foundations.* Council on Foundations. https://cof.org/content/effects-family-culture-family-foundations

Roth, J. (2018, August 15). *Are you a shopaholic? How to fight a shopping addiction.* Get Rich Slowly. https://www.getrichslowly.org/shopping-addiction/

Royal, J. (2024, May 1). *14 passive income ideas to help you make money in 2021.* Bankrate. https://www.bankrate.com/investing/passive-income-ideas/

Schwahn, L. (2023, July 7). *13 ways to find the best deals online.* NerdWallet. https://www.nerdwallet.com/article/finance/best-deals-online-shopping-tips

Snoop money-saving app. (n.d.). Vanquis.co.uk. https://www.vanquis.co.uk/manage-your-money/manage-with-snoop#:~:text=Snoop

Stanger, T. (2024, April 16). *Lower your home energy bills right now.* Consumer Reports. https://www.consumerreports.org/home-garden/energy-efficiency/lower-your-home-energy-bills-right-now-a1457706663/

The benefits of upcycling. (n.d.). FutureLearn; FutureLearn. https://www.futurelearn.com/info/courses/upcycling-for-change-from-green-ideas-to-startup-businesses/0/steps/67684

The importance of expense tracking accountability. (n.d.). FasterCapital. https://fastercapital.com/topics/the-importance-of-expense-tracking-accountability.html

Travers, M. (2023, June 28). *5 mental health rewards of embracing minimalism, according to A psychologist.* Forbes. https://www.forbes.com/sites/traversmark/2023/06/28/5-mental-health-rewards-of-embracing-minimalism-according-to-a-psychologist/

von Aulock, I. (2024, April 23). *Differences between short, medium, and long-term financial goals.* Invested Mom. https://www.investedmom.com/blog-2/short-medium-and-long-term-financial-goals

What to do with extra cash: Smart things to do with money. (n.d.). U.S. Bank. https://www.usbank.com/wealth-management/financial-perspectives/financial-planning/extra-cash.html

Why Frugality is an important part of personal finance. (2024, July 16). GoKapital. https://www.gokapital.com/why-frugality-is-an-important-part-of-personal-finance/

Williams, G. (2023, March 27). *10 best personal finance courses.* US News & World Report; U.S. News & World Report. https://money.usnews.com/money/personal-finance/family-finance/articles/worthwhile-online-personal-finance-courses

Wilson, D. (2020, May 26). *The secret to leveling up in life? Finding your marketable skills.* Medium; The Post-Grad Survival Guide.

https://medium.com/the-post-grad-survival-guide/the-secret-to-leveling-up-in-life-finding-your-marketable-skills-53dcb56cb5ec

Wong, K. (2016, August 3). *How I manage my income as a freelancer*. Lifehacker; Lifehacker. https://lifehacker.com/how-i-manage-my-income-as-a-freelancer-1784732927

www.ingramcontent.com/pod-product-compliance
Lightning Source LLC
Chambersburg PA
CBHW071133050326
40690CB00008B/1450